SURVIVAL

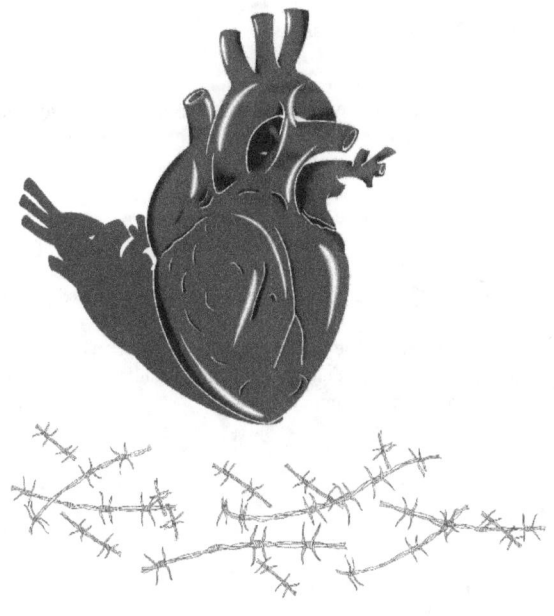

Magesoul Publishing

A TRILOGY OF ANTHOLOGIES: BOOK 2

SURVIVAL

Copyright © 2020 Magesoul Publishing

All rights reserved. No part of this publication may be reproduced, distributed or transmitted in any form or by any means, without prior written permission, except in the case of brief quotations embodied in critical reviews and certain other non-commercial uses permitted by copyright law.

This is a work of fiction. Names, characters, places, and incidents are a product of the author's imagination. Locales and Public Names are sometimes used for atmospheric purposes. Any resemblance to actual people, living or dead, or to businesses, companies, events, institutions, or locales, is completely coincidental.

Each chapter and contents are the author's works. All alterations have been subject to author consent and approval. Formatting and presentation have been completed with the author's preferences in mind.

Publisher:

Magesoul Publishing
PO Box 580019
BRONX, NY 10458
www.magesoul.com

Editor: Nat White
Assistant Editor: Lauren Radey

Book Cover & Illustration Design: Adric Ceneri
Interior Format and Design: Adric Ceneri & Nat White

ISBN: 978-1-953786-01-2 (Print Version)

INTRODUCTION

The human mind is a powerful tool.
The soul, our best guide.

In times of adversity, we need to become masters of both.

When faced with hardship, trauma, and suffering, we can experience some of the ugliest and most negative of human emotions. The often lonely and deeply personal process of survival forces us to look beyond these, no matter how hopeless a situation may seem, and rise.

Within that process, as our true capabilities are realized, we often discover they are nearly always greater than we give ourselves credit for.

Following on from "It Hurts", this second anthology in Magesoul Publishing's first ever trilogy, delivers a collection full of grit, courage and determination, as an outstanding group of 25 writers share within their own personal chapters, what it took, what it takes…

To survive.

TRIGGER WARNING

This publication includes content related to trauma, pain, loss, and suffering, a proportion of which, may be considered violent, graphic, or distressing to some readers. As such, reader discretion is advised.

If you are triggered and require support, you are strongly encouraged to seek help from your personal support network or reach out any one of the agencies listed below:

NATIONAL SUICIDE PREVENTION LIFELINE [USA]:

1800-273-8255

INTERNATIONAL ASSOCIATION FOR SUICIDE PREVENTION:

https://www.iasp.info/resources/Crisis_Centres/

...

CONTENTS

Introduction --- 003

Contents --- 005

PAIN TO POWER - Alicia Young --- 007

SURVIVING THE BLOOD IN MY VEINS - Jorge Anton --- 017

THE SUM OF ME - Lois Rose Sterling --- 033

I LIVED AND I'M ALIVE - Cedrik O. Wallace --- 041

SELF-LOVE IS A BATTLEFIELD - Frollein Fleckenstein --- 049

TRANSFORMING MY HATE - Adric Ceneri --- 069

FOR THOSE WHO DON'T THINK THEY'RE GOING TO MAKE IT
Angela Marie Niemiec --- 085

FATHER - Kristin L. Provenzano --- 093

ENDURANCE - Tyrell Tinnin --- 101

BREAKING FREE FROM MYSELF - Shefali Dang --- 109

SURVIVING THE FALL - Nicole Gabert --- 117

YET I LIVE - Karlye. S. --- 133

STAY TUNED FOR THE ENCORE - Chris Faenza --- 141

FATHER SUN, DAUGHTER MOON - Cynthia Hallynn --- 149

LONELINESS - Sakshi Narula --- 165

THE REMNANT - Cass Marie --- 173

CONTENTS [Continued]

181 --- Joe Steele - SURVIVING SUICIDE

195 --- K.M. Lennan
      ONE, TWO, THREE, FOUR... I DECLARE A SURVIVAL WAR

223 --- Dena Helmer - BARE BONES

239 --- Alex Le'Gare   TADASANA

247 --- Nat White - NO PARACHUTE

271 --- David John Smith - ATTEMPTS AT LIVING A REGULAR LIFE

287 --- Callie Carroll - OPEN WOUNDS

297 --- Carlos Medina - INTERNAL

307 --- Casandra Rojas - IN SEASONS

319 --- Books by Magesoul Publishing

321 --- Books by Carlos Medina

322 --- Books by Adric Ceneri

323 --- Magesoul Publishing books by other Authors

325 --- The Trilogy of Anthologies

Pain to Power

ALICIA YOUNG

ABOUT THE AUTHOR

Alicia is a mother of two who resides just outside of Toronto, Canada. She began writing in late 2016, but finally found her stride in 2018. She writes about life, love, heartbreak, motherhood, and sensuality.

Alicia has made a name for herself on Instagram; her work has been shared on many feature sites and by those who are touched by her words. Her work has been published in three books available on Amazon and she is currently working towards publishing her own collection.

   @nutmeg_and_maplesyrup

SURVIVAL

Fraudulent

When old demons appear
I rock back and forth and hum old spirituals
because only God knows the storm raging in my soul
When the pain becomes unbearable
and I can't contain the onslaught of tears
waiting to flood my face
I stretch my arms way up and yawn
just in case I need to justify the red in my eyes
When manic and depressive collide
I draw a hot bath with bubbles
rose petals and music
all conjured to mask the weeping
as I cradle my knees to my chest
and scream with no sound
It's a bit fraudulent I know
but I do what I must to get through
I'm a survivor

SURVIVAL

∷

Anxiety

I carry anxiety with me every day
I hide it under head wraps
with plastic smiles
red nail polish
and in the outer pocket of my designer purse
It sits with me
overpowers me
whispers at night when all is still
and I'm most vulnerable
It pounces
sits on my chest then tries to suffocate me
It is unpredictable like Friday evening traffic in July
and as comforting as a bed of coals on the sole of my feet
It is a silent monster
a manipulator who has convinced me
to keep our interactions a secret
It is seducing
reducing me to a lesser version of who I was meant to be
It tells me I'm out of control
It tells me I'm going to pass out
It tells me
I
am
going
to die
It tells me to alienate
It tells me to sanitize
It tells me to stay home

SURVIVAL
It is irrational
sporadic
intense
menacing
and oh so manipulative
Sometimes I burn sage
Sometimes I chant Psalms 23
Sometimes I sow tears
with hopes of reaping happiness
and on days like this
when its fragrance overpowers
I crawl under the heather grey blanket gifted to me
and sleep

SURVIVAL

Turning Off the World

I'm turning off the world
I've been carrying her load for some time and I'm tired
It seems inappropriate while history repeats itself
and chaos walks the streets
but I need someone to take me to the place where love lives
someone to calm my fears
and reassure me everything's going to be alright
I want him to taste the fear and anxiety on my trembling lips
trace hope on the small of my back
and worship the mahogany skin the world rejects
but I feel so beautiful in
I want him to kiss it softly
so softly it sings in harmony and no longer feels like a threat
I've been enraged for so long
stoic so long
screaming so long
so tonight, I'm going to lower my voice to a whisper
and surrender

Tripped

I tripped and fell face-first into hurt and disappointment
I ripped the knees of my jeans
bloodied my nose
and knocked the wind out of my unsuspecting soul
I laid on the cold concrete for a while because my legs
were uncertain
they didn't know where to go
but I knew
I had to get up
I had to pick up the debris and wipe dust from my eyes
You see
I loved a man who saw my strength as his weakness
He whittled my worth to naught
skewed my thoughts then beat my confidence into
submission
A man whose sweet lies seeped through my innocent skin
and stained me
A man who faked his death just to see if I would cry at his
funeral
A man who convinced me that the tenderness below my
navel was my only carriage
I spent alone moments wondering
why the one who bore the pain of my birth never one day
uttered love
never patted my back
never felt proud

SURVIVAL

> Why the one from whose seed I sprung didn't know my
> fourth-grade teacher's name
> when I became a young woman
> and if the pain in my belly was hunger or abandonment

I was two little pills from the white light
the pearly gates and halos when I envisioned the beating of breasts
heard the wailing and all the unanswered whys
I left behind
I sobered from my emotional stupor
caught my tears in my palms and waited for the sun to rise because
I had to get up
I worked my fingers to the bone for decades for folks donned in Cartier cufflinks
and generational wealth
desperately trying to convince them that my wage doesn't cover the cost of everyday living and telling them of the many sleepless nights flipping dice contemplating which bill to pay
There were days when I stifled the intruding voices
days I faltered and forgot my faith
days when I had to remind myself of the courage and carnage of my ancestors
and Carmen Hercules' blood flowing in my veins
I had to get up and remind myself that someone somebody loved
didn't make it through the night
I had to get up and stand in my power
I had to rise

They Asked Me

They asked me how I made it
How I made it through the valley
with wolves disguised as sheep
How my upper lip remained stiff
when every bit of me trembled
How I carried pain and made it look like confidence
How the splintered pieces of pride lodged in my throat
didn't suffocate me
How I kept my dignity intact
after crawling on my belly
searching for pennies
begging for mercy
How I waded in waist-deep water at day's end
clutching to the wrist of my eldest
while balancing the youngest on my back
They asked me how I stood tall with the weight of
motherhood rounding my shoulders
How I handled those hellbent on staining me
with the stigma of single mother
and placing all the ills of society in my womb
How I made it to every game
every concert
every meeting
every
fucking
thing

SURVIVAL

They asked me how I made it
but I can't explain
so I turn my head to the sky
fill my lungs with the grace
mercy and abundance
pouring plenty from heaven's cup

Surviving the Blood
In My Veins

JORGE ANTON

ABOUT THE AUTHOR

So, who's Merlin?

A New Yorker, born and raised in Queens, Merlin is a visual artist and a writer. He's been writing since he was fourteen, when his English teacher convinced him to join the Poetry Club as extra credit or fail her class.

Merlin's writing has not been influenced by any specific poet as he has not and does not read any poetry books. Instead, he prefers to let his mood swings and life situations influence his work, considering his writing a mix of emotions brought on by his bipolar thoughts and schizophrenic tendencies. Because of this, you will find he writes in various forms and subjects of poetry, from the innocent and romantic to the extremely dark and suicidal.

Also a visual artist via his photographs, he tries to combine both art forms as best as he can using his photos to inspire his writing. Other times, he'll write a poetry piece and go in search of a picture to capture a scene for it.

"They say a photo can tell you a thousand stories and it is true, they can, but sometimes they just need someone to tell it for them."

  @iamjustmerlin    @just1merlin

  JustMerlin.JA

I stare
at this
whiskey bottle
nightly,
hoping the
infusions
of alcohol
poison my
bloodstream
and take me over like
an overdosed Pooky;
"beam me up Scotty"
and deliver
my poisoned soul
into another dimension
of forgetfulness
as I drink to
forget you
and survive
another night
of nightmarish
lullabies singing
to me reminders
of what you've done.

Let the drink
bury my existence
into a dark oblivion
as my humanity
falls apart
at the mere sound

SURVIVAL

of your name,
which sadly
carries the
same sound
as my own.

and though
I was not
named in
your honor,
I carry with me
all the dishonor
of being your son.

You see,
my mother
once told me,
she never thought
I'd be the one
to turn out
like you,
and yet,
here I am,
a reflection
of the one
I've expelled
in full rejection
from my life,
you.

SURVIVAL

∷

"Aye carajo,
this isn't the fucking key"

And so
the day began
with a reason
for a beating.

"Dame tu llave!"
("Give me your key!")

All I did was ask
for my key back
when you were done,
but you made sure
to remind me,
nothing in this "home"
was mine;
it was all yours,
despite you
not putting
a cent in
towards
a single item
within these walls
I was forced to call
my "home".

SURVIVAL

You slapped me
across the face
like a handball
getting cut
for an attempt
to get a kill;
and get that kill
you did.

Every fatherly touch
you gave me,
put in the same sting
of a hornet stinging
the charred remains
of my heart.

Your "love"
came with
an abusive touch,
which felt more like
a fisting through my heart
and your taking a piece
of my soul
with every beating;
the brutality
of the discipline
you felt was required
to silence the
"rebellious" tone
in my voice

and make kneel
the insurgence
of my soul.

But you failed sir,
you see,
with each
striking lesson
you beat into me,
you taught me
to be better
than you;
why would
I become
the animal
you released
on me
when all you wanted
was to be
free of him
too?

SURVIVAL

∷

A first shower,
gave you this
power
to bury
in me
the pain
and suffering
brought on by
your own
traumas.

You felt you
had access to
control my life;
a living puppet,
one you didn't
need to feed,
except for
lies.

"Touch right here.
Point your finger
and twirl.

See?
I'm missing
what you've got,
so fill it in with,
your fingers.

SURVIVAL

Good,
now put your...

no honey,
look at her,
and put your mouth,
r... i... i... i...ght here.

Now,
stick your
tongue out
at her,
because
she's not
letting you
go in deeper
but someday,
maybe you will."

You
showed me
the ropes
and placed
a shadow
on the
immoralities
of each lesson.

Shadows
keeping in
the dark the
maliciousness
of your lessons.

```
SURVIVAL
```

Lessons full of
painful reminders
I buried long ago
in the sepulchers
of forgotten traumas
except for those moments
when the whiskey goes dry
and ages in the barrel
of arduous remembrance:

God, please wipe
these shit-filled cracks
in my memories
clean enough
to believe they
never happened.

But these
memories
pull through
from the seams
of lies I tell myself
to survive:

These things
never
happened,
did they?

Maybe,
they're just
bad dreams
of a past life.

SURVIVAL

And so,
I awake hoping,
I've survived
the poisons
in your teachings
and replaced them
with pleasures
every time
I look
to satisfy
their needs.

Dirty lessons
unable to be
cleansed
by the showers
of ecstasy
they cast
upon me;

waterfalls full
of their gluttony
demanding for more
as I try to get by
with no life rafts able
to get me across
the river of stones
they leave in the
wake of their
pleasured cries
begging me
not to stop.

SURVIVAL

You showed me
how to swim in
their rocky rivers,
but failed to give me
guidance on staying afloat
within their hearts.

Then again,
what would
a five-year-old child
understand about
love anyway.

SURVIVAL

⋮⋮⋮

From the
darkest day
of my life
emerged
a fighter;
or maybe
just maybe
this is
something
I tell myself
to remind myself
I am still here
surviving
and you are
not.

You took
the misguided trust
of a thirteen-year-old
and introduced
bitterness
into my soul;
I hate
the fucking world
and god can go…
yeah well…
he knows my heart.

Stupidity
led to a lesson learned
while bathed in blood.

SURVIVAL

Open wounds
and gushing
lacerations
showed me
my shame
and from those
rose the fires
burning my heart
to a hardened gem
with a burnt view
of life;
marred by the ashes
blinding my heart
from love,
showing me
there is no
such thing
as love,
but there is
survival…

and so,
that is all I do…
survive.

SURVIVAL

I am lost in my thoughts
and wondering to myself:
am I really lost or just drowning in
these shit-stained memories?
Rusty memory banks
poisoning the flow
of my thoughts
with waves of
yesterday's
bloody tears,
leaving my soul
drenched in the pains
I carry with me
today.

I bathe
my memories
with alcohol
in hopes
of getting them
drunk enough
to fuck off
and give me
a night of peace,
but instead
they rejoice
in my suffering.
Tell me,
why do you
smile at my
fucking pain?

```
SURVIVAL
```

Is it you
or is it me
smiling
at my reflection,
telling me:
"You fucktard,
you are standing
here in life,
whereas
he is not"?

But why is it
I carry these
pains with me
everywhere and
every fucking day?

The only response
I can wheedle out
of the reminiscent
catacombs found
in my poisoned mind:
I need them
for my own survival,
as they serve me
with doses of torment
to remind me
I've lived
through far worse
than this bullshit
life is serving me now.

The Sum of Me

LOIS ROSE STERLING

ABOUT THE AUTHOR

Lois Rose Sterling is a writer located in the Metro Atlanta area in the state of Georgia. She holds a bachelor's degree in Art History with 3 publications in academia. She has also published two collections of poetry within the last year.

When she is not writing, Sterling is a photographer, wife, and special needs mother to her beautiful daughter, Norah Jane.

   @thetasteofmypen

Handkerchief

I often look in the mirror
Not by way of vanity,
but to lock eyes with self to ensure my flesh
is still affixed to bone
So long weathering spells
of flushing sustenance from my gut,
breathing out words of blood,
keeping handkerchiefs close to the breast
The marrow of me,
dusted with missing blossoms,
canines, molars and incisors all groaning
as I stretch a tired mouth skyward
For I reek, of haunting
Mirrors, are no dwelling for a ghost…

SURVIVAL

::::

Fracture

I am present,
for a precious few moments of daylight
Sowing half-pulses to root-rot gardens,
herding blooms to bloodied wrists
Scents of funereal lust,
undercurrent of my breathing
A coven of bones devoted to my fracture,
and I curse my bondage to ivory wings
Deliver me death, and you breed a saint

Harlot

Harlot of the bleak,
I exorcise seeds of a swelling black from my core,
beckoning floral remnants from beyond my grave
And I am not dead
I am not, dead, though legions of decay dwell in my flesh
My charred windpipe still chanting in faded white,
before the clouds melt from my tongue
Invocation to the gates:
"I was an angel once..."

SURVIVAL

Beauty Mark

What am I but a broad in black?
In my defense, it started at six, where betwixt my lips,
gospels of the River Styx were fixed
But to look for light was to piss off my ghosts,
I coughed up hope, I scoffed at soap,
there's no washing that shit off when a girl's been groped
Still clad in shadows, I'm always mad though,
forever sad, so I didn't mope, no I coped with smokes,
purity revoked, this pale flesh is a joke
so I'm cloaked in smoke
Didn't waste time with blokes, only praying I'd croak
26 years of black, there's still flashbacks,
a soul full of cracks, there's no getting her back,
no bouncing back, no coming back, no back-track,
I'm a maniac with backpacks of paperbacks of prose
stacked like soundtracks not held back
Don't ransack my thoughts please
I'm hardly the bee's knees, so diseased,
so displeased with a life seized,
heartbeats freeze by ten degrees
Weaving prose is my expertise
Heart from chest, my escapee
What am I but a broad of dark
Your question mark
Soul, disembarked
Life put in park
And nighttime is my amusement park,
so today I make poetry my beauty mark

Mecca

Dying as I live
This is reality
Mere feet from a plague's appetite
Home, my perpetual pistol assassin-inn
Stampedes of the hopeless,
feeding on scraps of a medicine Mecca
Surviving on the extravagance of falsehood safety
Dust touches and shadows of embrace
Posing a farewell kiss to the here and now
Where the dawn is a fairytale known only,
as once upon a time...

Wretched

Putting out cigarettes on my thoughts,
I am a half-silhouette of throat-caught forest
Scripts and songs and requiems all snuffed out,
for there must be more than writing and rewriting strife
in the same day
My head, a small house where the dark enters casually,
making the sunlight scarce in all rooms,
yet the flowers endure
Who deciphers beauty from the wretched?

I Lived and I'm Alive

CEDRIK O. WALLACE

ABOUT THE AUTHOR

Cedrik Wallace started writing poetry in 2014 after his fight with Multiple Myeloma, a blood cancer. Decades earlier, whilst studying communications, social work, anthropology, and education at Whittier College, he dabbled in writing as a feature editor's assistant and a column writer for the college newspaper. Since becoming an educator in 1995, Cedrik has continued to work with students to this day as a Dean of Student Discipline and a Crisis Team member for the Los Angeles Unified School District in Los Angeles, California.

Six years since his journey with poetry began, he has been featured, published, and voted "Inspirational Instagrammer of the Year". Now a self-published author, his two books 'Why I Cry Burgundy Tears', and 'It's My Write' are available for purchase on Amazon. In 'Survival' Cedrik picks up right where he left off in his chapter 'Lived', from the first book in this trilogy, 'It Hurts', telling the story of how he mentally and physically survived the pain he endured while battling Multiple Myeloma. Forgiving the devil he battled and defeated, he enlightens us on how his journey with cancer is comparable to that of the coronavirus pandemic. Life after cancer is all about developing a new mindset, 'Survival Mode'. To survive and maintain remission is to live life with new norms and particular safeguards. Cedrik's words go on to describe a moment he realized that survival meant more than just waking up. In his words, *"It's not always heartbreak and pain... survival can inspire art."*

 @poeticsoldier   @cedrikwallace

 @booksbypoeticsoldier   @booksbycedrik

SURVIVAL

⋰

I forgive,
but will never forget the devil
for what it did while it lived inside.
After I forced it
to stoop to my level,
I defeated it and I survived.
I'm finally waking up
from a nightmare and
beginning to understand why
I continue to survive
this health scare.
I have a story to share.
One of self-healing
and encouraging self-care.
Where the devil burns
in his own fire,
the angels fly from above through
clouds of smoke, to inspire.

- I lived and I'm alive

SURVIVAL

::::

I've seen how it hurts many when
adjusting to this new way of life.
For me, I'm eight years into this fight.
The pandemic did not make me panic.
Self-isolating, staying at home,
taking extra precautions, and self-reflecting.
This is nothing new.
For some time now, Happy Hours and
other social gatherings have been limited.
I've been trying to keep my distance.
It was hard working at a school.
My coworkers were forever telling me
to wear a mask and spray Lysol.
I was staying away from all
with even a cold and staying home
when I came down with the flu
knowing I'd be quickly taken out due,
to me no longer being immune.
They say to straighten the curve,
following these guidelines is
supposed to be the answer.
If that's the case, I should be good.
I've been able to maintain many years
of survival during my life after cancer.

- *Not the new norm*

SURVIVAL

Hurting for so long,
survival became my only option.
If not, my soul would rot and
my mind would start to wander.
Returning my mind and body
to where it began, a time
where I almost gave up.
It was a moment I'll never forget.
That rocky bottom I had hit.
With uncertainty
I was struggling to fall,
if that makes any sense,
but it was harder to get
up and stand tall.
Bam!
I fell as I stood from
my restroom stall.
Passed out, I'm awakened by a
a first responder after a frantic call.
During my short stint of hospitality
came a moment of clarity.
It was then, I woke up, mentally.

- 911, a wake-up call

SURVIVAL

::::

It may have been
in my blood,
but beating cancer
was also in my blood.
Not to be cocky or rude,
but "Bring it on!"
became my attitude
as I walked around
with my chest up
saying, "Let's do this!"
to all those around me,
including nurses and doctors.
Ready to take on each day,
all of the ups and downs,
each battle, and every punch
that came my way.
I was determined to stay.

- *With confidence*

SURVIVAL

Feeling emotionally and
physically six feet deep,
underneath the earth.
Up and down.
Back and forth.

Not content
for what it's worth,
I squirmed my way
through the dirt
to reclaim my birth.

For those of you that know,
know it hurts.
But the survival of such pain
brings a sense of rebirth.

Enhancing the value
of one's self-worth.

- New lease on life

SURVIVAL

::::

Dead man walking,
at least it thought while stalking.
From it, I ran like hell
as it loudly yelled,
"You can run but you can't hide!"
So far so good,
because I continue to strive.
If cancer returns, seeking to find,
on full display
will be the fight of a lifetime.
For again I will survive.
In the meantime, I will heal.
Finding and defining my purpose
of being alive.

- To be continued...

Self-Love Is A Battlefield

FROLLEIN FLECKENSTEIN

ABOUT THE AUTHOR

Frøllein Fleckenstein grew up as the youngest of three in a small town in western Germany. From birth, she was surrounded by books, thanks to her mother who was an avid reader and shared this joy for books with her children. Words, the way sentences flow and the rhythm of dialogues fascinated Frøllein Fleckenstein from early on.

At the age of twelve, she began writing her own poetry. Some years were rich in inspiration, some poor, but there was always something to write about. Over the years she experimented with different styles - even some song lyrics can be found in her collection.

Writing has now become the best way to release all the emotions that stir inside, and with every poem she hopes that at least one person is moved and encouraged to keep on fighting. For it may feel as though we are alone, but we poets know we are not.

 @frolleinfleckenstein

The Battle

*I've taught myself to be the one
who's easy to leave.*

The nice one.
Who's easily approachable.
Who won't be mad
if you don't call for months.
Who will talk to you as though
we spoke just yesterday,
not last year.
Who is never too clingy.
Never intrudes.
Who always asks if it's okay
for me to share
an ounce of my pain,
ready to back off immediately
if you show even an inch
of disdain.
The one you can always come to with your problems,
but never burdens you with mine.

*I've taught myself to be the one
who's easy to leave.*

Easy to be left behind.
I tried so hard not to wound your world -
but you hurt mine.
Every problem you ever told me,
I weaved into a prayer for you.

SURVIVAL

My heart cried for every tear you lost.
Every happiness you experienced,
it sang with joy.
And then you left.
And it's my fault, because...

I've taught myself to be the one
who's easy to leave.

To never let others know
how much I depend on them.
How much I ache to be by their side
every minute of every day.

I learned the hard way,
that people start to loathe you
when you love them too much.
So I made myself approachable,
kind and easy to leave.
If they leave anyway,
at least they shouldn't leave with regret.
At least one of us should be at ease.

I've taught myself to be the one
who's easy to leave.

Now I wish I'd taught myself to hold on to someone,
'cause I want you to stay so badly,
but I don't know how.
I don't want to impact your decisions,
so how can I even ask you anyway?

SURVIVAL

This logic makes no sense, unless
you stay by your own choice,
not influenced by anything I say.

But the part of me responsible
for holding on, broke.
And although I put it back together again,
it creaks and groans.
No longer the perfectly set machine
it used to be.

It only allows me to be the one
who's easy to leave.

So please, if you read this:

Don't go.
Please.
I wish you could stay by my side.
Hold me close, don't forget me.

For I may be easy to leave,
but I don't know
if I´ll still be here
when you come back.
Your leaving may be
the last hit my heart can take.

You can only repair
something so many times,
until it's infinitely broken.

SURVIVAL

And I don't know, but that may be the one thing
we'll both regret the most.

*I may have taught myself to be the one
who's easy to leave.*

But I hope you'll be
the one who dares

to stay.

The Aftermath

Sometimes I wonder
if anyone hears
the 'I hate myself' hidden
behind every
'I'm perfect."

I wonder
if anyone sees the fear of losing
the last parts of me,
masked beneath
every smile I keep.

I wonder
if anyone feels the broken glass
that slits my soul in pieces,
if anyone tastes the ashes
that litter the air from my burning mind.

I wonder if they care enough -
to try to see behind.
Or if they're fooled by the grin -
or the happiness
I hide myself in.

I wonder why they can't see the tightrope
I balance on,
the one I'm scared of falling from -
while constantly telling myself :
You can fly.

SURVIVAL

(Maybe someday I'll believe that I am able to touch the sky.)

After all,
if you really want something enough,
it can come true -
or so I've heard.

But right now I just want someone, anyone,
to look me in the eyes and say:

"I've got you.
It's okay to throw away your smiles.
Release your fears,
let your anger roar.
It's okay to allow your hurt to flow.
Scream at the top of your lungs,
and know, I'll stand right here
and hold you until fear loses its grip.
Until your anger boils dry,
and hurt, is given to the wind.
I'll hold you close and tell you:
It's okay."

Because, *it is.*

And for once,
I don't want this person to be me.
I don't want to be the one
holding myself up high.

I know I can.

SURVIVAL

For the longest time – I have.
But I'm tired.
And sometimes I want
to let someone else carry the load.
Just for a few hours, maybe minutes.

Just to see, I'm not alone.
Because surely I am not
the only one I can rely on in this world,
but sometimes
it feels an awful lot
as though…
I am.

SURVIVAL

\:\:\:

The Reconstruction Planning

My hurt is not your poetry.

My pain is not a tale.
My wounds are no fable
for you to narrate.
My blood does not flood these lines to be analyzed.

My hurt is not your poetry.

And it never was.

It's hurt.
It's pain.
It's suffering.

Yes.
I know there are poems about it.
I know, I've written them.
But they are not tragically beautiful
or beautifully powerful
or powerfully brave.
They are not created
to leave you in awe
of my strength,
only to then turn your back
and forget.

My hurt is not your poetry.

SURVIVAL

It only flows into prose
because crying doesn't seem enough.
Talking doesn't seem enough.
Screaming doesn't seem enough.
And written words seem to be
the only words people trust.
I can tell them a thousand times.
I only have to write it down once.

So no...

My hurt is not your poetry.

For you to understand me,
I hide it in beautifully crafted words
that make the sting softer,
the edges smoother
and the blades blunter,
so my pain does not slice through your skin.
But let me make this clear:
I have been cut.
I am bleeding.
My scars are not yet healed.

There is nothing poetic to see here.
So don't stand there
watching and telling me
how courageous I am.
That you admire how well
I've dealt with the pain.
I haven't.
The ache,
is still very much there.

SURVIVAL

My poems don't cut you. I've dulled the knife
so no one else bleeds.
You should be grateful
that I have put
my hurt,
my pain,
my suffering
in words that will not kill.

Because believe me-
they would if I let them.

But my hurt is not poetry.
It is hurt.

My poetry is where my surviving starts.
It's my way to deal with the agony I've suffered.

My poetry is healing.

Not always for myself.
But maybe for you.

My poetry is healing.

My poetry.

Is healing.

The Reconstruction

We need to talk.
Yes,
I'm afraid it's necessary.
Yeah,
I know you don't want to.
But we need to.
I love you.
I truly do.
But this?
It's destroying you.
I know you may appear healthy.
I do.
You're not anorexic, not too fat, not lying in bed for weeks.
You smile. Go to work.
But, love.
It's killing you.
And not slowly over eighty years.
You will be dead in barely ten.
Although it may seem invisible on the outside,
inside, you are drowning.

Darling.
It's okay.
I'm not accusing you of anything.
I know how hard you're fighting.
I can see that.
But I also know that it's not enough to keep you alive.

Honey.

SURVIVAL

Love.

Yes, I know you hate to ask for help.
Because somewhere along the way you learned
that seeking help means you're too weak on your own.
That it means failure.
It doesn't.
It means you have more strength than ever.
Because giving a piece of your heart to another
and trusting them to protect it,
is the bravest thing you can possibly do.
And I understand
that it's also the scariest thing I could ever ask of you.

Lovely, please.
Do it.
You will see,
it's so much simpler
when someone else knows your pain
and offers to carry it for a while.

It won't magically disappear.
But more often than not,
you'll discover the wall you were trying to break down
for such a long time
is from another point of view, just a door.
And the key is hanging around your neck.
It's been there all along,
you just forgot.

Let other people remind you
of the wonders you carry.

SURVIVAL

Please love.
Please.

Let's live together for a long time.

Sincerely,

Your Heart

SURVIVAL

::::

A New Home

My body is no cathedral.
Don't try to worship it.
Don't praise its high ceilings,
its colorful stained-glass windows,
its golden interior.
My body, is no cathedral.

My body is no home.
Don't try to slip between my ribs,
tuck yourself beneath the curve of my spine,
or sleep between the living breaths of my lungs.
My body, is no home.

My body is no temple.
No God lives here.
No virgins will sing Her praises
and no offerings will burn their lives to the sky.
My body, is no temple.

Don't try to make my body something it's not.
It's simply a body:
two feet connecting me to the earth,
two strong legs carrying me everywhere,
a belly that's not flat,
but perfect for laying your head upon,
for it's as soft as a pillow.

My body is just that.

SURVIVAL

A heart only beating for me,
lungs who never take my breath away.
Two arms, the perfect length to reach out to someone in need.
Two hands, that handled everything the world has thrown at me so far.
A head that's sometimes up in the clouds,
but trying its best to keep the demons inside and out, at bay.

It's a body with
eyes that I've seen every sunset with,
a tongue that's savoured all the spices of this world,
skin that has kept all the veins and bones and organs and air and water and blood inside,
while creating a picture of me for everyone else.

I say it's not your temple, for there is no God.
But I am the God of my body.

I say it's not your home, for you can't live here,
but it's been mine since before I was born.

I say it's not your cathedral, so don't worship here.
But I worship it. It's mine.

It's bruised and scarred,
and more times than not, too big for myself,
but it's mine.
If it were a cathedral,
there would be gargoyles cackling on the roof.
If it were a home,
there'd be wind whistling through some broken windows.

SURVIVAL

> If it were a temple,
> there would be weeds breaking through the floor.

But thankfully, it's not.
It's just a body.
And although I don't always like it very much, I love it.
For it contains something holy.

Me.

And that was a difficult lesson to learn.
That this body is worth something
even when others don't see it.
So I honor it.
So should you.
Love your body.
It contains something holy.
You.
And if that's not a reason to worship,
I don't know what is.

Transforming My Hate

ADRIC CENERI

ABOUT THE AUTHOR

Adric Ceneri is an artist, poet, writer, and author. He writes about his sexuality, the events that marked him throughout childhood and the difficulties he faced when he was growing up. Ceneri often writes with a rebellious heart through his poetry, expressing his emotions and always remaining true to who he is as an artist.

As a poet and writer, he transmits his feelings and embodies his transgressions in magical wordplays, truly transforming pain into art. Adric's four journals and his books 'Walking Towards Happiness' and 'Caminando hacia la Felicidad', are available on Amazon.

As Marketing Manager and a home author for Magesoul Publishing, he is also the creative genius behind the covers for this trilogy, 'It Hurts', 'Survival' and 'Healing', among other books. His books 'The Remains of a Human' and 'Los Restos de un Humano' are available now.

@adricceneri   @booksbyceneri

@adricceneriwrites   @adricceneri

www.adricceneri.com
@adricceneriwrites

Neglected

I can no longer hold these tears in my eyes,
the pain in my soul and the hatred in my heart.

As I grow older,
I can only feel the void growing inside.
Because when I was younger,
when I was a child, I was neglected time after time.

Today, as the adult I am,
I understand why things happened the way they did.
But the inner child in me…
can never understand.

I *survived* the ignorance
of countless people who hurt me.
I had to endure the pain on my own,
not because I didn't trust telling my parents,
but because they weren't there for me at all.

A part of me will always feel abandoned,
unwanted, unworthy
and never quite fitting of this life.
Even if there's joy around me,
nothing will ever fix the damage done
to my brave heart.

SURVIVAL

:::

Corrupted

He corrupted my childhood,
tainted my heart with sins and salacity.
He took away my innocence.
He was the adult, and I was his sex toy.

I feel violated on many levels,
and I don't know how to feel whole again.
I feel robbed and abused with every breath I take.
I feel angry and nothing will ever be the same.

I enjoyed the fervor; I enjoyed his flesh.
I let him touch me because I thought it was love.
I didn't know any better, and I was lost.
I didn't have parents, and I wanted to be cared for.

I was only eight when my mind was forced to transform
into an adults.
I felt different— there was perversion in my thoughts.
I grabbed onto his world that offered corrupted love.
I craved love, compassion and warm hugs,
but I exchanged them for sex, blowjobs and lust.

I no longer wanted to play with toys.
If it wasn't him I was playing with, I felt bored.
I was preyed upon for being lonely,
for not having parents or a home.
No child should ever have to endure what I lived.
I have walked a few miles on the darkest roads,
but I *survived*, and I wear my scars as I bare my soul.

Divided

I'm sad and angry, feeling completely out of control,
losing parity to the suppressed emotions inside my soul.
I have collected dark memories and tears of joy,
I've hidden every broken piece that made me whole.

For decades, I listened to the bible readings of the Lord.
I hated myself for what I felt as I learned it was wrong.
It felt good being attracted to other boys,
yet it was a sin according to the Bible's words,
or the interpretations of those humans filled
with regrets of their own.

I became angry with myself
for concealing my emotions for far too long.
I felt things that came naturally to my body and soul,
but I felt trapped by their teachings
and my never-ending thoughts...

My recollections became nightmares
and I was the host.
I am tired of the burden I have carried all along.
I am sick of the society who let me pay the cost -
a society that turned a blind eye and closed its doors.

I am tired of hiding the shattered parts of my angry soul.
I am tired of remaining quiet, and I no longer wish to run.
I am prepared to live and die for what I am at any cost,
to set myself free from these chaotic thoughts.

SURVIVAL

I am ready to let go.
I have endured so much hurt for so long,
but now I don't want to feel it anymore.
I have ***survived***, and now I want to live and enjoy.
I want to feel alive and I am willing to let
my demons explode.

SURVIVAL

In Darkness

Pushed to the point of breaking more times
than I could ever say or recall,
I learned to love the darkness
and appreciate its cold.
There are dark places that I wandered to get lost,
but not by choice.
The solitude and silence spoke louder
than my own voice.

I remember the first time
I felt anger raging in my heart.
I was five
when I witnessed my mom get beaten up.
I felt my heart when it leapt
out of its cage too fast,
as I threw a knife at
the alcoholic beast I called my Dad.
I was so young,
but even though I felt so hopeless,
I wished for it to slice
his guts wide open.

I remember the first time
I felt sadness wetting my eyes.
I was six
when she left for work just like
any other day,
except this time my mother left
and stayed away.

SURVIVAL

I waited long enough, only to see
my tears fall to the ground.
I felt so lonely and unprotected
without her around.
Feeling unloved and left behind,
the world seemed darker
on my side.

I remember the first time
I looked fear right in the eye.
I was seven
when I felt its shivers
running down my spine.
I didn't want to feel what I was feeling-
but I was judged.
Judged, for not being 'boy' enough.
I didn't fit into society's standards
or religious laws.
I lived in fear for years not knowing
it was okay
to be who I was.

I remember the first time
I felt abused and torn apart.
I was only eight,
and I'll never erase the hurt,
the tears, the scars.
The physical and emotional pain I felt
as he tore through my insides,
was a sorrow I tasted and endured again
countless times.
I should've never have had to live
through that disgusting, vile act.

SURVIVAL

I remember the first time
I felt lonely and ready to die.
I was twelve,
and all I wanted was a hug,
but all I got that awful day
was blamed for being late
and looking all beat up.
Feeling worthless,
I thought it was my time.
With 37 sleeping pills in my mouth,
I tried to exit this life-
swallowing one by one
as I let my tears roll down.
Feeling the amnesic effect of erasing pain
from the inside out.

I remember waking up confused
and tied down,
angry at myself for still
being alive somehow.
Empty and consumed
by my thoughts, too loud,
left with a bittersweet taste
of the life I'd thrown out.
I was still here,
and my mind was above
in the clouds,
wondering how I could possibly
continue living now.

I remember feeling miserable
for not being able to fit in anywhere.

SURVIVAL

I was fourteen,
and disappointing people became my forte.
In my attempt to eliminate my pain.
I jumped off my father's fishing boat
while it was running over the blue sea.
I felt a painful crash and then a release.
I gasped for air and then, salted water I seeped.
I swallowed too much water and I went under.

And as I began sinking,
I saw my life dimming away.
The rays of light under the water were fading
along with my accumulated suffering.
Sinking felt peaceful, somehow.
Absorbed by the darkness,
I was momentarily at ease.
I took a taste of the tranquility
I could never have had,
living in this deceitful world.
I remember waking up, at the seashore in the sand,
spitting salted water and taking another breath of life.

I remember I was bullied, but I didn't care anymore.
My soul was broken and I had nothing left to lose.
I grabbed onto my pain and embraced my beaten soul,
and shielded myself with the hatred from my wounds.
I did what I did to survive this treacherous world.
If death was not ready to take me with her,
I was not willing to allow ignorance to steal my joy.
I did not want to suffer their violence anymore.
I remember being mad,
and I still feel anger in my heart-
all this negative energy I collected over time.

SURVIVAL

I was fifteen,
the day I last saw my Dad.
For years I've examined our last fight.
He beat me up with a log of wood,
consumed by anger and his broken pride.
He found me having sex with another boy
and he simply couldn't accept that his only son was gay.
I stabbed him and I have never regretted that I did,
for it was either to save my own life
or let him murder me.
He acted outrageous- like a rabid animal.
So many times, I regretted leaving him alive.
But today I can say I did what I had to,
to **survive**.

I remember feeling
like a total outcast my whole life.
I was sixteen when I fled Mexico
and moved to the Northern Lands.
I thought it would be better,
I thought I would be happy at last
going back to my mother,
but she wasn't herself and neither was I…
We had changed through the years…over time.
I was no longer a kid,
and she didn't even know
what I had to endure
after she left me behind.
I felt trapped in a foreign world,
I felt afraid of the sounds in every sentence,
While my heart was submerging in turbulence,
the hurt inside my soul needed release
and I couldn't contain it.

SURVIVAL

Unfortunately, I was lost once again,
swimming against the current of emotions
in my heart.

High School was not a pleasant experience for me-
it was another test for me to pass.
I barely made it out.
I buried myself in books,
searching for the meaning of life;
only because I didn't know what life was.

I remember running...
searching for something missing in my life,
and I felt the void inside my soul grow emptier each time.

I was nineteen,
I traveled alone in a pitch-black dawn.
I traveled north to Maryland.
I was seeking what I didn't have,
something I never felt but that was missing in my heart,
a void that grew and almost ate me alive.
I remember going back to my mother's house,
and my body was changing.
I felt the clock of my heart.
I was twenty,
the clock was ticking...
and I was running out of time.

I ignored it, deciding to live.
I no longer wished to live, just to survive.
Alcohol, drugs and sex filled my nights-
countless promiscuous encounters with strangers,
picking them up at bars.

SURVIVAL

I remember meeting someone who was literally fire,
and I was gasoline waiting to be lit,
to burn along with everything in my path.
I was twenty-one,
I should've never forced that toxic relationship,
but I did and I paid the cost for striking the match.
Four years of intense darkness and needless drama,
four years of wasted emotions and never-ending lies.
Our fire grew out of control
and I played with it,
until it burned me for the rest of my life.

I remember I got sick with a chronic illness
and I knew what I had done.
I was twenty-five,
and I had no one to blame but myself alone.
I didn't need more sorrows.
I remember I was afraid because I didn't know,
but for the first time hope knocked on my door.
I learned to take care of myself
and to love myself, baggage and all.
I educated myself, and little by little
life began to let my dark clouds dissolve.

I remember meeting him, my love,
and I showed him every dark corner of my world.
I was twenty-six.
I thought of the possibility of him running,
and if he did, he wouldn't be the right man for me
anymore.
I knew somehow that if he was the one,
he would stay with me, despite my thorns.
And he stayed, and now we are an "us".

SURVIVAL

And just when I thought I was done with tests,
a major obstacle crushed me like a bug.
I remember, I felt it. I felt my heart— it stopped.
I was scared— I had so much to lose this time.
I was twenty-eight.
My heart murmur was failing me at last.
It was leaving me alone, breathless, and sad.
I needed repair, like a malfunctioning car,
I needed surgery, and they opened me
like in a science lab when students dissect frogs.

I remember opening my eyes.
I felt pain and I didn't know where I was.
I took a breath and I tasted life, like the first time.
I was still twenty-eight but I felt anew.
Reborn into someone better,
someone with scars and damages,
but with the opportunity to live
and enjoy the little things in life.

I am grateful to have ***survived***,
to be here and living, feeling fully alive.

SURVIVAL

Astray

There was a time in my life
when I wanted certain things I couldn't have.
For some reason, I've always felt
like I've lived thousands of years and out of place.
The beginning of my life was painful
and filled with the uncertainty of countless tests.
I am a ***survivor***, living proof of what I faced,
but I no longer wish to survive— I want to live instead.

As a child, I was wronged by ignorant minds.
I was judged based on their morally questionable acts.
I was the victim of predator who tore me apart
and I was treated unfairly every time,
as if I was at fault for being who I was.
As if it was my fault my parents left me in their town,
as if I wanted to be flamboyant
so that other boys could bully me for it.

I wanted to belong, to fit in somewhere,
but that never came to pass.
I was meant to be different but I was lost and alone.
My parents, without knowing, left me to my own luck.
I didn't have the love and support I needed
and I crawled toward sinful and immoral acts.

I don't know how to explain the archaic feeling,
the ancient essence that illuminates my thoughts.
My spirit feels the joy of a never-aging child,
and my mind has the wisdom of an immortal soul.

SURVIVAL

I have come to terms with who and what I am,
and I no longer pray, for my faith in God has left a void.
I am a sinner who believes in his every cause.
I am not big on second chances anymore.
If you hit me, I will punch you back.
I believe in karma and its debt-collecting laws,
but I prefer to fight for what I believe in at any cost.

I've grown tired of my silence from this world
and I will voice my opinions as I stand tall.
Life has challenged me and shaped me strong.
I took beatings, psychological abuse and sexual assault,
and it's time to place the shame where it belongs.

I am a *survivor* of what I couldn't control,
a *survivor* of countless painful wrongs,
a *survivor* of ignorance and neglect all along.

I am a *survivor* and I will remain strong,
but I am tired of hiding behind closed doors.
I am tired of the silence I have carried in my soul,
tired of hiding the truth as I hold my tongue.

I am going to live, and this time I won't care.
I will face my demons— for I am no longer scared.

SURVIVAL

⁝⁝⁝

I Survived

I came into this world,
and from the beginning I fought for my life.
I felt my mother's love,
and all of a sudden she was gone.
But I *survived*.

I yearn for the parents that left me behind,
for love from the family I never had.
I felt broken and my heart turned dark,
and my hatred became my shield to stay alive.

I took shelter under perverts who used me like a rag.
I buried my soul deep under their lust,
and allowed them inside me as they moaned.
I was lost, living in lies.
And every night I would cry into my pillow,
but I *survived*.

I wished for healing
and a pardon that would never come.

Years passed but I was stuck in that awful place,
playing this game of never-ending lies.
Then the drugs made me sink to a deeper hell,
and I drank away my life.

It didn't matter what I did or didn't do,
I was damaged and there was no cure.

SURVIVAL

Nothing could fill the emptiness in my soul-
all of my hopes had died.

But during one of my sleepless nights,
crying over my pillow,
my heart stopped.

I woke up, still among the living.
And for a split second I thought I had died.

I tried taking my own life but didn't succeed.
One million forbidden sins were my escape
to a reality my soul was never able to take.
And I took every punch the world ever gave,
but no one ever noticed my dreadful pain.

I didn't know what I wanted;
I only knew what I didn't need.
And with the strength of my hatred,
I picked myself up off the floor.
I swore to run, to run away from these lands,
even if that meant being forgotten,
because I got tired of living like this,
and my fear evaporated like smoke.
I ran away to ***survive***.

And ***I survived***.
I faced the fears and the darkness, all at once.
I felt liberty for the first time in my life.
I took a taste of what freedom was like,
and there is no way I am going back.

For Those Who Don't Think They're Going to Make It

ANGELA MARIE NIEMIEC

ABOUT THE AUTHOR

Angela Marie Niemiec sees life through poetic eyes. She turns dreams into poetry, while her writing reflects her experiences. Inspired by strong connections, poetry is her way of bridging the gap between the lonely soul and pure human connection. It's that bond that is the key to opening her creative side; resonating with others is the bonus.

Often riddled with metaphor, her poetry is her escape from reality. However, even when writing about the darkness, she has a way of still holding onto the light, and you will see this in her poems. Instead of remaining in the grips of victimhood, she will raise you to empowerment.

Her premier book, *Once Around the Halo*, published in 2019, is a collection of poems on a spiritual journey to find healing while overcoming chronic illness, loss, and heartache. Since then, she has been published in an art book and a half dozen unique anthologies worldwide.

   @angel_writer

SURVIVAL

⋮⋮⋮

Dear Survivor

Have you ever stared into a mirror so long
that you no longer recognized your own reflection?
...while counting the fractals behind your eyes as you realized
all the lines you memorized faded into a lie of *I'm fine*.
Have you ever squeezed your fists so tight,
tracing the skin on the back of your hands,
following the ripples that cracked and bled,
shifting from triggered to split from white-knuckling it?
Have you ever screamed so loud
you caused your own ears to ring?
...while veins bulged from temple to temple,
filled with the sound of mad blood pounding through
for all to hear, it's never been more clear,
it's time to *get the hell out of here*.
Have you ever thought you just can't go on,
that life is just a long and useless journey of pain from hell and beyond?
...but all along, you've belonged,
because what caused you to wear down and nearly break
gave way for you to rise up, stand tall, strong and brave.
Now, do you recognize your strength?
That force inside that keeps your going,
causes you to never give up no matter how intense the pain.
That very thing pushes you up every steep hill,
guiding you to the top of each goal and dream,
always inside you, a companion to grace,

SURVIVAL

>   waiting patiently for you to recognize it each and every day,
>   it's your strength for survival,
>   and no one can ever take that away.

∷

Breaking Silence

Never give up,
never give in
and never stay silent.
Silence keeps you controlled,
control is how they stay in power,
power instills fear,
fear is what keeps you there.
This is how they try to dominate you
and all your thoughts;
they don't want you to think for yourself,
because then you might uncover the truth.
You might rise up,
find your voice,
take your power back,
and then,
they'll lose.
This is why
you should never stay silent,
never stay down,
always speak up
and never give in.

SURVIVAL

Outsmart the Enemy

They'll try to contain you,
but you won't let them catch you.
They'll try to clip your wings,
but you'll just fly higher.
They'll try to declaw you,
but you'll just scratch deeper.
They'll try to file down your fangs,
but you'll just bite harder.
They'll try to tape your mouth shut,
but you'll just scream louder.
They'll try to tie your hands behind your back,
but you'll just swing further.
They'll try to blindfold you,
but you'll be able to see through,
because no matter how hard they try,
you'll try harder.
You won't let them win,
because you
*are a **survivor**.*

SURVIVAL

::::

It Just Goes Blank

Crying in the aftermath
of a broken glass scene,
screaming,
pleading for life,
to stop it all,
please!
Clawing, gnashing,
tearing the sheets,
face down in a pillow
to muffle the screams,
but no matter how much
you begged it to stop,
you kept being told
to just "shut up"...
Curled up in a ball,
tears streaming down your face,
you push all those haunting memories
so far away,
to the point that
it
just
goes
blank.

SURVIVAL

Head Above Water

Learn to swim,
said the voice from within,
treading through a dark sea of tears,
while the rapid currents try to pull you
down into the undertow.
Learn to balance,
keep your head straight,
ears back and chin up high;
that is how you float,
face up, soul to the sky.
While the gravity tries to pull you apart from the reality,
learn to breathe,
while choking on memories
in a haunted closet full of skeletal parts,
hands around the throat,
muffling the sound of a bleeding heart.
Learn to be strong,
in a world trying to constantly weigh you down,
compounding weights tied over your back,
while shackled ankles shorten your tracks.
Learn to be aware
of those who don't know how to swim,
they will take your humble ounce of kindness,
turn it into an ocean, and then blame you
when they drown in it.

SURVIVAL

::::

Karma

Sometimes you just have to wonder,
after it is all over,
when is their turn to suffer?
When will *what they have done to another*
get to happen to them?
Will it be here on earth,
in a prison cell,
or deep down in the pits of hell?
You see, it's not that we should wish bad things upon others,
or purposely want to see them hurt,
but I think we all know...
that's how karma works.

Father

KRISTIN L. PROVENZANO

ABOUT THE AUTHOR

Kristin Provenzano was born and raised in Akron, Ohio. She started writing at a young age and had her first poem published in high school. Inspired by some of the toxic relationships she had been in over the years, Kristin fell into poetry – sharing her experiences in words, in hope she would in turn help others face their own ordeals, with the knowledge they are not alone in this world.

Kristin wants people to realize it's ok to talk about what has happened in their life, and that we are all in this together.

 @kristin_l_provenzano @provenzanokris1

 kristinlprovenzano

SURVIVAL

Maybe in another world
I would be important to you
How I view men, my well-being -
would be your priority
You would want me to see
how a real man is with his family
Someone who is around
Shows up
Doesn't lie
Never raises a hand
How I wished for that so many times
For that person to appear
To know what it really means for a father
To love his daughter
Sadly
The only important one in your life is you
Even after all these years
You're still at the top
And I'm still at the bottom

SURVIVAL

∷

As I have gotten older
Flashbacks of you came back
The screaming
Hitting
Hiding scared
Though I have forgiven you
I have become more sensitive to it
It breaks my heart to see how a father treated his little girl
I think of when I have kids
I could never
Would never
Inflict that upon them
The fear you must have seen in my eyes
Yet you never cared with each hit
Did you ever feel anything inside after that?
Or were you just dead?
Making me feel your wrath

SURVIVAL

⋮⋮⋮

I have always known deep down
You would never change
This facade you portray
Only fools the outsiders
If they really knew you
The real you
You're so good at hiding it though
Making it seem like everything is perfect
I have always seen who you truly were
Even from a young age
Those rose-colored glasses never worked on me
That's why I chose to keep my distance from you
Knowing that if I got too close
I would burn again
Sitting in a pile of your bullshit
That you love all too much to create

SURVIVAL

My grandfather was an amazing man
The love he gave me
Words couldn't describe it
All you saw was your father
Your issues with him always took center stage
You never wanted him to love me this much
Jealousy ran off of you
I will never understand how someone's father
Would never want their daughter
To have a loving relationship with their grandfather
You tried to poison my mind
Said all these horrible things about him to me
It never worked
My grandfather was still my hero
He always will be
You though,
Shame on you
Trying to keep us apart
When you knew he was getting older
Not wanting him to have love from me
You will never compare to him
He showed me unconditional love
What it would be like to have a real father around
He will always be that person
Who sits in my mind
With love beating from my heart

SURVIVAL

I sit here contemplating so much in my mind
Once again
Here we are with you
With words said
Actions you took
There actually was a chance
That presented itself for you
To stand up
Be that father
You so clearly announce that you are
Of course you chose wrong
Like you always do
Now I'm left with
A pit in my stomach
Can't sleep
Or eat
Realization this most likely will be the end of this relationship
There's no going back
You made your bed
How can I ever forget the things you said to me
I can't just turn a blind eye
Those words cut so deep
Wounds that will stay open
As a reminder for me
You're never going to change
You are who you are
And with age
Sometimes you don't get better
I never wanted to be that person
who cuts a parent out of their life

SURVIVAL

But now
There'll be more damage done to myself if I stay
I have to accept who you are
Forgive what you have done
Be free of you for good
Because love does not hurt
And fathers
Are supposed to be our protectors
Not the monsters hiding in the closet

Endurance

TYRELL TINNIN

ABOUT THE AUTHOR

Tyrell Tinnin is an artist, poet, author, and father living in Wichita, Kansas. Inspired by a creative writing assignment during his freshman year of high school, he has been writing stories and poetry for over two decades.

After publishing a novel in 2008, he found himself unable to write anything significant for years. Work, life and fatherhood left little room for much else, until years later, when his marriage fell apart and he turned to poetry to work through the toughest time of his life.

To this day, Tyrell sets aside time to write.

 @tyrell.tinnin tyrell.tinnin.3

Survivor

Here I am, alone again at the end of everything
This waxing moon has left me forever wanting
You never know what the dealer has yet to deal

The fates were kind this time, letting me escape
And I found myself standing on this lonely road
You never can hold back the tide in the end

I try to heal, but end up reopening the wound
My hands weren't built for such delicate work
You never see the real damage you've wrought

Someday I hope to find a safe place for my soul
But today I'm thankful to survive another day
You never feel the full weight of your own heart

SURVIVAL

:::

The Path

My eyes still water when I think of our life
But I gave you back all the stolen moments
My wounds still leak through my bandages
But I bound the pieces of my heart together
My hands tremble remembering your touch
But I've stopped looking for you in my sleep
My lips still quiver at the thought of yours
But I can no longer taste you like I once did
My body longs to feel warmth in my bed
But you're not the one I imagine anymore
My soul will always hold a place for you
But it is only a sliver of what it used to be
My skin aches to be touched by soft fingers
But your long fingers are now a stranger's
My world gets a little brighter every day
And my body and soul heal with the light

Roar

It took a long time for me to stand up
To find my feet after years of kneeling
To find my voice after too long a quiet

But some didn't like the power I found
They'd grown accustomed to the old
And didn't know how to handle the new

It may be rough and raw, but it is me
I won't apologize again for who I am
Or for knowing what I want out of life

I am only human, full of flaws and sins
I know I will stumble, slip and fall
But I'll keep getting up again and again

My heart will always be in the right place
And I'll protect myself and those I love
And never let my roar be silenced again

SURVIVAL

::::

Endless

I feel a little lost sometimes
Adrift on this endless sea
All my tether lines severed
And my moorings slipped
Now I wander and wonder
What is to happen to me?

Endless possibilities await
As do endless dangers
No real sense of direction
And no way to steer anyway
The moon offers little help
And the stars have quieted

Floating toward the horizon
Slash of black against navy
Rolling with the tall waves
Ready for whatever comes
Adrift on this endless sea
I feel a little lost sometimes

River Rock

I am a river rock
Tumbled and tossed
Smoothed over time
I endure the storms
I survive the floods
And one faraway day
When this body is
Smashed to pieces
And cast all about
As sand or pebbles
I'll go on enduring

SURVIVAL

Typed in Flesh

No matter what I use
Or how hard I scour
I cannot wash off
These fucking scars
They are far too deep
And too entrenched

Their roots dig down
Wrap around bone
And entangle muscles
After too many failures
I eventually gave up
Trying to remove them

So instead I scrub them
And polish them up
Let them shine brilliant
In a new day's sunlight
Learn to acknowledge them
And honor their power

These scars are a story
Typed into my flesh
Edited by only time
I cannot ever hide them
So I will share them
And turn pain into strength

Breaking Free from Myself

SHEFALI DANG

ABOUT THE AUTHOR

She wrote her first poem about a 'Silly Goat' who lost his fur coat when she was in grade eight, for her younger brother's school project. That's when Shefali Dang discovered her love for words and ability to rhyme, and that when the two came together, they could create beautiful stories and vivid imagery. Going on to write for her school magazines and school competitions, no matter what she did, her love for words stayed the same.

Shefali lives in Toronto, Canada, with her husband and two children. A self-taught photographer, she enjoys reading and immersing herself between the pages of a good book. Her creativity is not limited to the arts, she also loves cooking and trying out new recipes.

With very few knowing of her passion for writing, when she started sharing her words on the Instagram platform almost three years ago, many were surprised to discover her hidden talent.

She mostly writes about life, love, and healing.

  @theshefalidang   @shefalidang

Finding My Way

*I'm praying for the clouds to part
and the sun to come shining through.
I'm waiting for the light
to scare the darkness away.
I want to come home to myself.
I just need to find the way...*

SURVIVAL

I Can Finally Enjoy the View

I drank so many cups of coffee,
sitting lost in thoughts of you,
thinking I was found,
but I was a fool
and had no clue.
I didn't know then that darkness does not come announced,
nor does it come with thunder and gloom.
It can walk into your life with arms open wide,
flashing a bright smile
and before you know it you are doomed.
Now I know better.
I might even call myself a warrior.
I cried, I screamed, I gasped for air.
Then I dug my way out from there.
I grew and bloomed and grew.
And now that I am where I wanted to be,
I can finally sip my coffee and enjoy the view.

Between the Dark and Light

Some days I wake up feeling swollen
from all the darkness bloating inside of me,
my fragile joints buckling
while my body crumbles from within.

Some days I wake up feeling light,
like a cloud floating in the skies.
Soft as breeze, effortless as breath,
but strong enough to weather all storms.

And I know,
it is in between both,
the dark and light,
the fragile and strong,
that I will find myself if I look hard enough.

Growing Pains

I collapsed under the weight of it all,
crashing into myself, drowning deep within my shell.
I couldn't carry on anymore -
So I let it happen
the sinking,
the breaking,
the crumbling,
the undoing.
Thinking this, was the end.
Little did I know,
this unbearable pain
was just me breaking free from myself.
I was growing and I needed more space to stretch and bloom.
My old shell wasn't enough anymore.
My world was evolving,
my soul expanding
and my heart did what it does best -
it kept on beating,
teaching me
to love myself once again.

Getting Ready for This Beautiful Life

The mountains
that once seemed too steep
to climb
now look like mere pebbles.
The gallons of tears I shed,
both day and night,
now seem vital in the cleansing of my sight.
Every heartache was just that,
a pain of growing into myself.
All those times I felt my world had collapsed,
it was just me shedding another layer.
I understand it now.
I was getting ready for this beautiful life.

SURVIVAL

⁝⁝

Living Isn't the Same as Being Alive

It took me time to learn
that darkness isn't meant
to be feared.
How can I fear something
that already resides inside me?
It is meant to be understood, befriended and moulded.
It would be unfair to say,
I need it to go away,
because there are many lessons
to be learnt
in the absence of light.
It taught me to fight,
to survive,
to thrive.
It taught me
living isn't the same
as being alive.

Surviving the Fall

NICOLE GABERT

ABOUT THE AUTHOR

Nicole Alyssa Gabert has always considered writing to be an inherent part of who she is. From the moment she put pen to paper, she fell in love with the written word. As a child, she began creating short stories, and her interest in literature never ceased. Yet, Nicole's love of poetry only began four years ago, after discovering it when becoming part of the Instagram writing community.

Currently the Associate Editor of Instagram's Poetry Battles, a platform which hosts online worldwide poetry competitions, she is the Poetry Battles Champion for Game 2 (2018) and Game 19 (2020). Most recently, Nicole has joined the Magesoul Publishing family as an Assistant Editor. Her work has been published in Wildflower Warriors, an anthology aimed at bringing awareness to the crimes of domestic violence, sexual assault, and rape. All proceeds from this collaborative project were donated to the victims of a domestic violence/rape shelter for women.

A New Jersey native, Nicole currently resides in Pennsylvania with her 14-year-old daughter, and their two beloved cats, Spike and Jade. As a New Jersey special ed pre-k teacher, she has found her love of storytelling and poetry to be a way to connect with the children in her classroom. While her poetry touches upon a wide spectrum of subject matter, all of her work is tied to her belief that we are all here together, as spiritual beings, having a human experience.

 @nicole444_fallenangel   FallenAngel

⋮⋮⋮

/The Survivalist/

In desperation, I crawl forward
from the depths of this
mad, mad world...
The light before me reaches forth,
an *e x t e n s i o n*
of beautiful brilliance,
begging me to fight the darkness
which threatens to take hold of my being;
pull me into its realm,
reign its dominance over me,
enslave me within its prison...
And yes, I know I am supposed to
just keep moving ahead.
Do not pause.
Do not stop.
Do not listen.
Yet, fear grips hold of me,
whispering doubts
over and over into my ears...
That I am weak,
that I am far from worthy of
such beautiful things...
Mesmerizing me,
with its demonic lullaby.
And sadly, I find comfort in a song
so familiar.
I am the battlefield of a holy war
between

```
SURVIVAL
```

my ascending spirit

and my broken mind.
With great force,
each pulling me
in opposite directions,
until I am ripped in two,
torn *o p e n*,
and these poetic words bleed endlessly
from my tortured soul...
And I, am tired...
I am so exhausted
that I am running out of ways
to make them sound so beautiful.
And it, is all my fault...
I am the reason
this life has grown stagnant with indecision.
And I, am just trying to survive
in the creation
of my own
d
  e
    s
      t
       r
         u
           c
             t
               i
                 o
                   n.

SURVIVAL

∷

/Broken Compass/

I am lost,
somewhere in this great big forest…
So tired from chasing
that part of myself
that somehow
slipped away
when I wasn't looking.

Confused,
because I thought myself capable
of navigating these trails
without any map,
thoroughly convinced
I knew the terrain
by heart…

Yet here I lie,
caught beneath the underbrush…

At first believing
this entangled mess
would eventually work itself out.
Then, finally accepting
it wouldn't.

And I have grown numb here,
in this foreign place.
And I am so tired,
that I only wish to close my eyes.

SURVIVAL

Perhaps,
in dreams,
I shall find my way home.

/Isolation Weighs on These Bones/

Isolation weighs on these bones,
grown weary from the exhaustion of
just another day on repeat.
Naked and vulnerable,
I collapse into the corner and fold
into the empty spaces of me.
Bare skin pressed against
cold tile walls,
this empty shower stall
offers no comfort
to a soul deprived of human connection
for far too long…
The Darkness
crept in slowly;
an unexpected visitor
an uninvited guest.
As Monday
bled into Sunday,
bled into Someday,
among the rest.

Isolation weighs on these bones
and I feel myself disappearing sometimes.
Lost, between day to night,
night to day,
though time's just an illusion,
anyway…
Shadows play upon the wall,
as all my demons come to call.

SURVIVAL

Whispering as I close my eyes,
all their satanic lullabies.
Sadness
spills
into every part
of me...
And I only wish to kill the pain,
to quiet the voices,
or go insane.
So, I'll swallow down
these antidepressants,
curb Covid's psychosis,
political infection.

Isolation weighs on these bones,
and slowly convolutes my senses.
A prisoner inside this home,
entombed within these catacombs,
And how is it I am to imagine a future,
when I cannot see past the view
from behind my windowpane?
Darkness seeks to eradicate
all knowledge
of what humanity was,
for the re-education
of what it is, to become...
It strips me of all I know to be true.
And I find myself here,
curled into a ball,
bare skin pressed against
cold tile walls.

SURVIVAL

Isolation weighs on these bones,
and Darkness pours itself upon me,
like a second skin.
It steals the ink from my pen,
and holds it hostage, laughs,
and demands my sanity as ransom.
I lift my palms in silent prayer,
as it drips itself against my veins,
begging me to inject it
into my bloodstream.

"Let me in, and I shall become your addiction..."

Isolation weighs on these bones,
and Darkness seeks to
blind my vision
of a better tomorrow,
to infect the air I breathe
with the bitter flavor of toxicity
It demands of me:
Do not feel.
Do not see.
Do not hear.
Do not taste.
Do not breathe.
Let the memory of your humanity
fade to black.

Isolation weighs on these bones,
yet Darkness, so consumed
with a need to
possess my physicality,
fails to see the salt I've spilled

SURVIVAL

upon the floor,
or smell the sage that burns
on the counter,
only
    inches
        away...
It does not realize that this space,
bare skin against
cold tile walls,
is my church.
And beneath the water
is where I pray.
It forgets that I am so much more
than this human form...
My spirit rises from within,
an oceanic tsunami crashing against the shore.
Shadows that swirl upon cold tile walls
drown beneath the color of my aura...
Darkness retreats,
and with conviction,
I demand the return of all it has sought
to take from me...
My soul has never been placed
upon my altar
as an offering to a lesser God.
The ink, that runs through the blood
in my veins,
has never been available
for the taking.

Isolation weighs on these bones,
yet, I reach my hands above my head,
grab hold of the faucet handles,

SURVIVAL

and turn them 'round.
Until the water flows from above,
and covers my skin like rain,
cleansing me of the sick
and twisted lies
that only wish to infect me,
like the virus itself...
I watch as Darkness swirls below me,
and disappears down the drain
until the water runs clear.
And I remember-
I am both the mother and the daughter.
The poet and the dreamer.
The Chinese dragon that breathes passion's fire.
The starseed that glows
the color of the ocean.
I am the medieval French herbalist,
once condemned, and born again...
And the many lives lived before
and after that one.
But, most of all,
I am the embodiment of love, kindness,
and pure intentions.

The weight of isolation falls away,
if only for the moment...
and I find my way back,
to self.

SURVIVAL

/Miraculously/

And, I prayed for a miracle.

And, if prayer
is supposed to
work so well,
then I didn't
understand
why everything
continued to
crumble around
me, except... *so much faster now!*
And, as I stood in the middle of my chaos,
where the sky was falling,
the air was escaping and the walls were closing in...
It was then, *that I knew...*
God had shown me
the truth.
God had
shown me
my strength.
For, when
everything
lay in ruins,
at my feet...

I was still standing.

Miraculously.

/The Reason/

The hourglass falls in the field of dreams.
And the sands of time scatter
in every direction.
A nightmarish reality begins to
unfold before our very eyes.
And we, stand frozen,
in momentary disbelief.
"Tell me this isn't real!"
Fear weaves its way in between,
and around,
all of the words you whisper.
And my only wish is to protect you
from the chaos approaching.
From this madness,
gaining momentum,
with unpredictable,
insurmountable speed.

The hourglass falls in the field of dreams.
An earthbound collision,
its glass shatters upon impact.
The sands of time spiral into a carousel,
spinning and spinning.
Closer and closer,
the storm races toward us.
Before the shotgun signaling start
is fired...
Before the red light turns green...

SURVIVAL

Before the word, "Go,"
has the time to escape anyone's lips...
And we are told to *just stand still.*

"Tell me this isn't real!"
Anxiety paints your plea with desperation,
as I hold on to you tighter.
And my only prayer
is to be your shelter
from this raging storm
that begins to surround us.

The hourglass falls in the field of dreams.
Yet, when the clock stops,
we're told time is of the essence.
So, amidst the cataclysmic destruction
of the only truth we have ever known,
we fall to our knees,
and pray to a God
we don't understand.
"Tell me this isn't real!"
Comfort seeks a home in the response
you long to hear from me.
My only instinct is to hold you closer
when words fail me.

And, it is now, in this moment,
where there is only you and me,
that everything becomes crystal clear.

And, I tell you, with innate knowing,
"Do not be afraid!"

SURVIVAL

The hourglass falls in the field of dreams.
And broken bits of glass break
through the illusion of what we thought mattered,
to immediately reveal the truth of what does.
2020 vision redefines clarity,
and a childhood memory rushes in,
reminding me of a gift that somehow,
I let slip away through my fingers
as time surpassed the innocence of youth.
The image of a seven-year-old me,
at an eye exam
where 20/20 surpassed
the minuscule 1% at 20/10,
settling on 20/5,
and, suddenly,
I had the power to see further
than anyone the doctor had come across before.
His voice declaring,
"You are a rare phenomenon!"

And so, finally, I assure you
that none of this is real...
That the only "real," in any of this,
is you and me...

And, as the world crumbles,
and the storm rushes in,
we stand together...
and turn our eyes to the night sky,
which looks exactly the same
as it always does...
And it reminds me of something...

SURVIVAL

Something I must've forgotten,
in this lifetime or the last one,
or the one before that...

And fear is absent from your words
when you ask me, wide-eyed,
"How is it that we are still standing?"

And with love, I tell you,
"Because, this world, this new world...
This is the reason we are here..."

Yet I Live

KARLYE. S.

ABOUT THE AUTHOR

Karlye is a poet, photographer, and jewelry maker. North Carolina born and raised; she enjoys being outdoors in nature.

An Instagram poet since 2018, she is often referred to as K.S. or Mama Shakespeare by the poetry community. Her favorite thing about writing is that she can relate to almost anyone or anything, drawing a close connection between writer and reader. Writing everything from short stories and humorous pieces to long form poetry and lyrics, her style varies from day to day.

Karlye has a very unique signature style, her pieces are typically full of metaphors and layers of symbolism, enabling the reader to interpret them in multiple ways. This not only allows them to come to their own conclusion, but upon revisiting, uncover a new perspective each time.

  @mamasshakespeare

Self-Preservation:

My father is a psalmist; he sings his lines aloud,
reverberating melodies into the sultry, dim light.
His psalms, written in condition, like the scars
that line a robe of flesh, draped on the dark days
of its warfare. He shouts glory into the bitterness
which fogs the daydream view; as wool, pulled down
over our eyelids is only to shield us from the sight
of our own brokenness.
The sweetness of his song
fosters sweat drops on the back of my neck. A hum
of salvation from these days of doom, a psalm as
covers these evil ages; like gravy pouring over a bed
of rice, seeping between the cracks. His shouts of
love begin to mend the cradles in his soul, a wounded
heart that was once bitten by a terror in time, now is
blanketed, bountifully, and by no means of self-
happiness (my father tells me, through his song).
But this- this is self-preservation.
A psalmist of the bleating hearts,
a single song in a dying breath:
his own survival, and that (my father says)
is why he sings.

Memories and Unfinished Dreams:

I bought a pair of newborn socks and a little toy horse,
gave them to the woman, heavy with child,
who walked down the street.
It seems that these days,
you live most through the empathy in me…
or perhaps it is me, vicariously living (thriving)
on a respirator
of coiled and collected, unfinished dreams
that you have left me with.
Baby blue blankets?
I'll take three, just to fill my arms with these "could-be's",
(Though I move them on quickly).
If the hurting means giving away a part of me,
I will take the pain, the storms and the rains,
for I live and I breathe, connected to you,
merely living off of a respirator,
filled with memories and unfinished dreams.

SURVIVAL

⁙

Death (of Life):

I tug at the skin on my lip,
peeling the deadness until it bleeds.
I tug at the loose fabric of my heart,
tearing open a wound that has never
fully healed. Blood spits down onto
the ground. Let it spill. Let the others
behind me see my trail, the crimson drool
that rests itself on the bed of earth.
May the buzzards circle all around me,
pick at my eyelids while I am still awake;
until I bleed. And then, let them find me.
Let the beasts of the mountains lick my wounds
and gnaw at my bone; but let those behind
me find me, sore and weary, broken-hearted
and abandoned, clinging only to the distant
thought of an afterlife with those who have
gone on before me, those whose trails I have followed.
Let them find me, those who pursue
this path after me. Heaving, gasping, but breathing.
Surviving. Not thriving, lest I take my next breath
for selfish ways to stay.
Let them find me, departing
into an ethereal realm. No, not perishing, not only
dying…but dying again.

And this time, dying, to finally live.

SURVIVAL

::::

Die:

"Die."
You said.
And I did.
I died a little more inside
each time you spoke to me,
each time my eyes met yours
after that day.

"Die."
You said.
And my confidence
fell into the coffin.
My ego dropped
lower than a thermometer
inside of your cold, cold heart.

"Die."
You said.
And the cherry tree of love,
once watered with hope in my heart
withered up and fell victim to the drought.

"Die."
You said.
And I didn't.
(That you could see.)
But I did, you just didn't believe.
So you killed everything

within me.

"Die."
You said.
And I did.
Again.
But something grew,
something lived,
a tree of hate, and it's for you.
And I didn't bear fruit,
but hatred, oh, it grew.
And your very voice watered it
every time
you said,
"Die."

SURVIVAL

::::

Maid Service:

A heavy whir of the vacuum as it sweeps across the floor;
cleaning up the mess. Blocking out the shouting of
yesterday's angry words between us... the ones that we
allowed to come between us.
A hum of suction aspiration as it collects tiny cells,
unplanned gatherings, swallowing whole and cleaning
our mess... the mess we made of a loveless eve.
The whirr blocks out the dream of life, held
in arms and intertwined in devotion, one much
unfit for the life our brokenness could now supply.
The wind, chilling me to my core, bones rattling
vehemently, reminding me of how it all was before...
I brush my hand across my cheek, with a whisper of
hopeful forgiveness: I remind myself that
I am cleaning my own mess.
It is a constant pool of pity, one that lies between
us and the dream we once had. Yet not all is
finished in our time, and it will be alright; for
we are never alone. We are all cleaning our mess...
not by means of being free... not by means of known
intentions... but by means of sheer survival.

Stay Tuned for The Encore

CHRIS FAENZA

ABOUT THE AUTHOR

Chris is a self-described word slinger from Northeast Ohio. His writing style has been most often described as bold, honest, and passionate.

A father of three, he enjoys cooking, painting, and reading poetry in his spare time. He self-published his first book "Words on Fxcking Paper Volume One: Lessons Learned in the War for My Heart" in 2019 and is currently working on a spoken word album.

 @wordsonfxckingpaper

(Prelude)

I want to know how
I'm supposed to
Grow from this, and thrive
How I'm supposed to even
Come out of this
Alive

I want to know how
I'm supposed to
Come out the other side
Stronger and better
When right now
I'm fucking STRUGGLING
Just to survive

SURVIVAL

(Introduction)

Mistakes are made
When you take your own feelings
In vain
When you forget to look
In the mirror
And realize that
You could be to blame

And this is the story of how it
All fell down around me
Again
Just when I thought
I'd found hope

And this is the story of how I
Climbed out of that pit
Alone
When I realized there was no one
At the other end of the rope

SURVIVAL

∷

(Rising Action)

You are a special kind of
Imperfection
The way your lips curl into a smirk
When you're happy
And the way you bite your lip
Almost imperceptibly when you're thinking
And the way you
E·nun·ci·ate
When you MEAN IT
And you want to make a POINT.
The way your eyes roll
The way your voice
Trails off sometimes
The way you pick at your fingers
When there's something bugging you inside

And I hear your voice in mine
And I hear your words in everyone around me
And I can't stop seeing you in the small moments
EVERY DAY
That I know you would
APPRECIATE
In ways that nobody else will ever understand

I keep falling
Farther in this hole
And I'm not sure
(Without you)
That I remember how to land

SURVIVAL

(Climax)

The air felt so thick
That I couldn't breathe
And it felt like the sky
Was closing in on me
Falling down all around
In
Patterns
Building
Walls
Protecting me from the storm
Or hiding me from
Everything

Possibilities
Tainted
Feelings drained
Intentions rearranged
And I was left to wonder
If the woman I'd loved
Had ever existed
Or had she just
Changed?

(Changeover)

Don't let go
That's the secret, I swear
And it's exactly the opposite
Of everything I ever learned before
But I had to realize
That these memories
These moments
Frozen in time
Are so much more

They are the proof
That the love I believe in exists
If only for small moments
But maybe that's enough
To give me the hope
That I need
To keep going
When I'm ready to give up

(Finale)

What remains is only insignificant evidence of your brief existence.

Memories of your brilliantly belligerent demeanor. Your tendency to stack syllables side by side into the night, never needing a sign but looking anyway, and always warning me that you would someday say goodbye.

I didn't listen.

I swore our souls were tangled, some type of unbreakable bond, the kind I never believed in - imagine that - I was right all along, and I think deep down I knew this was wrong. I let myself get carried away with accepting connecting with someone who was only half there, I filled in the gaps myself with the things I swore you'd swear (if you swore anything) and I made myself believe in a version of you that wasn't real, so no wonder I was so fucking surprised you would leave.

But since you've been gone, my mind keeps painting in the brightest colors - unfettered now, no expectations to live up to and no fear of falling down. I found my voice again and remembered how to speak my truth freely and take ownership of my identity. Truth be told, I think losing you helped me, find me.

Father Sun, Daughter Moon

CYNTHIA HALLYNN

ABOUT THE AUTHOR

Cynthia lives near the Blue Ridge Mountains in Virginia with her family. She has been an avid reader and writer for as long as she can remember.

She holds a Post-Master's Degree from The University of Virginia, where she received specialized training to work with adult survivors of childhood sexual abuse, victims of domestic violence, and in the treatment of trauma in general. She began sharing her poetry publicly in late 2018, when she began posting to the Instagram poetry community.

Since then, Cynthia has been published on several blogs and in numerous poetry anthologies. She is a curator and live reader for several IG feature pages. Cynthia says that much of her writing is informed by personal and professional experiences.

Cynthia feels that her most important role in life is that of mother to her two young daughters, who she is determined to raise to be strong women.

 @seasoundsc

Waxing Crescent

He swings her
around and around,
holding her by her long,
thin arms.
Her hair flies about her head
like a lion's mane –
"Again Daddy! Again!!"

she shrieks.
And so he twirls her,
he whirls her.
Once, twice more.
Not for a second
does she worry
that he might drop her.
*Daddies always protect
their little girls*,
she knew this to be true.

She smiles
as he places her feet
on the dusty ground.
Her eyes are twin twinkling, sapphire stars.
She is happy,
she is secure.

This is what it felt like to be four.

SURVIVAL

∷

Waning Gibbous

Even from here,
I can still see her there,
beneath the great oaks.

Only eight years old.

All gangly limbs and flaxen hair,
shining gold in the sun's light.
Meticulously,
she plucks one wild daisy,
then another.
Ties them together with delicate,
careful fingers
until they form a circle –
a crown.

She places it on her head,
wild little princess,
perfect picture of innocence.
Apple,
of her Daddy's eye.

I look away,
wish I could go back
and save her,
all too aware
of what awaits her.

SURVIVAL

The confusion she'll feel.
The sorrowful tears.

The "How's"
and the "Why's?"
My only solace,
the knowing…

She. Will. Survive.

SURVIVAL

∷

Eclipse

The first time it happened,
I was nine.

It was a night like any other
as far as I could tell.
You weren't home,
but that wasn't unusual–
you often worked at night.
I would sometimes
sleep with Mom.

Occasionally,
I would still climb
into bed with you both
after a bad dream
or if I heard a scary noise.
You both had always indulged me
and I felt safe in your bed…

I felt *safest* in your bed.

And it didn't seem
out of the ordinary at all
when Mom,
heavily pregnant and uncomfortable
on that ardent
August night,
made the fateful decision
to leave me
in the bed
she shared with you,

while she went to rest
in mine.

I remember
hearing you come home
sometime after that.
I was almost asleep,
laying on my side,
my back facing
your side of the bed.
You entered the room silently,
and climbed in next to me.

The first hint
that something was amiss,
was your hot,
sour breath on my neck.
Stale, bitter ghosts of the cigarettes and
beer
you had consumed earlier
in the night.
The odor was unfamiliar
and unpleasant.
You placed your arm
around my body
and pulled me close to you.

*Did you know that innocence can be
destroyed in a millisecond?*

Because it was in that instant
that my mind boiled over
and alarms started blaring in my head,
loud and angry…
"SOMETHING IS WRONG! THIS IS NOT OKAY!
WHAT IS HE DOING??!!"

SURVIVAL

As you started to touch me,
I felt myself leave my body
and float above to the ceiling, where I watched…
in shocked confusion,
then
with numb detachment.

When you were through,
you told me not to tell Mom.
You said I would just upset her.
You said it was our secret.
You said,
"After all, it wasn't that bad,
was it?"
You said you thought I was her.
You said *no one*
would believe me.

And I believed you.

I don't remember,
but I must have slept.

I woke up the next day convinced that what had happened
the night before
must have been my fault.
Over the years,
you convinced me
I asked for it.
The shame and disgust I felt
kept me quiet.
I mastered the arts of complacency and –
Compartmentalization

This was my new normal.

Overnight my entire
fairytale world,
my idyllic worldview,
were obliterated.
My body, a warzone.
My life,
capsized.

SURVIVAL

⋮⋮⋮

Waxing Gibbous

Well, it was bound to happen/ Eventually/ And I wonder if you thought about it/

I was sixteen/ I had my first/ /serious// boyfriend/ And the thing is/ He was four years older/ So this

one time/ He asked me/ "Who taught you to move like that?"// And I died// Except not really/

Because I had to keep moving/ Plus it wasn't his fault/ Because he didn't know/ No one did/

And I didn't know the answer to that question anyway/ Was it you? / It really doesn't matter

now / But once I was through moving //For him// I told him/ And he cried //*He cried*//

And maybe I cried too/ But maybe I didn't/ Because I was just numb/ And that didn't really matter

either/ Because I was only moving for him, anyway/ And after he cried/ he was so angry/

And I liked it/ He said he wanted to fuck you up/ /And I liked it /A lot/ Then a few weeks later/ You came to my bedroom door late at night//Again//

SURVIVAL

Like you sometimes did// On the nights//that Mom worked third shift// The door and the lock were a joke/ But I never laughed/

Nor did I sleep/ I just lay there//Waiting// But on this night, when I heard you/ Something

woke up inside/ And I screamed at you through the door// "*Leave me alone! **I'll fucking kill***

***you** if you ever come near me again!!*"// The words pushed themselves out of my mouth/

Almost toppling over one another/ They were racing to be said/ To be heard/

Like they'd been waiting/ For seven years// And they were through taking it lying down//

For good measure/ I told you what he had said when I told him//That he would fuck you up//

You stopped jiggling the loose knob with the cheap lock/ And went away/ The next day/ It felt

good/ thinking you were frightened/ Of me/ Or of him/ But not really// Because nothing ever

felt good// You stopped coming to my door after that/ And I was able to finally sleep//

SURVIVAL

Which is almost funny it's so absurd// Except I still can't laugh// Just like I still can't sleep/ But there

is one good thing/ That night/ I took the first step//*Towards taking my power back*// And I scared the '*fuck*' / right out of you

SURVIVAL

The Present

Dear Father,

The celestial metaphors have all
called out sick today.

To be honest,
I suspect they're conspiring against me
or have rejected me altogether.

Staying out of sight.
Somewhere Up There.

But, then again,
I learned long ago
that due to the mess you left of me,
it's not unusual
to jump to such conclusions.
Believing myself to have been rejected
at the smallest slight
or something altogether unrelated…
Having nothing whatsoever
to do with me.

So I'll just say
what I'm writing to say
straightforwardly.
Excusing their absences.

SURVIVAL

I forgive you.
I forgave you years ago.

First, for myself
and my own mental well-being
But now, for you.

Because I know
that you had it rough, too.

I am attempting to break
generational cycles.

And ancestral curses.

It is my hope,
that my daughters
will have less
to forgive.

And their children, someday,
even less.

But the main take-away
for you,
is 'I forgive you'.

So, now,
forgive yourself.
For I have tucked it all away.

Mostly…

But, yes,
forgive yourself,
because I already have.

Love,
Your Daughter

Addendum:

Dad,
If you're reading this now,
for the first time
or the second,
I guess you understand or soon will,
why I asked you
to read the last poem first
and then again
after reading the previous ones,
in the order they are placed.
Because it is
arguably,
the most important.
Though, to be clear,
they are all important,
because I have been validated
and taught to let go (mostly).
Taught,
if I wanted to survive
I would first
have to find a way,
to forgive.
This is the greatest gift
I could give to myself.
And to you.
I hope you recognize its value
and treasure it.
Always.
~ C~

Loneliness

SAKSHI NARULA

ABOUT THE AUTHOR

Sakshi Narula is the author of the celebrated poetry collection, 'Loveish' and the poetry series 'The Art of Staying Lost'. Born in New Delhi, India, she has since lived in over eight cities and three countries.

Passionate about art, travel, and culture, she finds happiness in writing and sketching. Sakshi's style of writing is simple, layered and easily relatable. Her love and sad girl poems are both empowering and heartbreaking short stories in themselves.

An active member of the poetry community on Instagram and Twitter, Sakshi started 'The Heart of Poets Foundation' to promote poets and poetry across social media platforms. Music, sketching, and cooking are some of her other passions besides poetry. She calls the beach and the museum her happy place. Sakshi currently resides in Muscat, Oman, with her family.

 @mssakshinarula   @mssakshinarula

 www.sakshinarula.com

 sakshinarulaofficial

Nuclear

What are they doing about the bombs now?
There are no more wars, I heard,
nothing left to defend, no rebel birds.
The streets are empty
and the graveyards buzzing with stories.
An era of human psychedelia has ended.
Gardens and backyards wait for spring,
and they keep waiting yet spring never comes or so it seems.
Can we even call it "spring enough" from inside these cages?
What did they do about the bombs
that they so proudly bragged about?
None of them better than a young girl in pubescence,
staring at her breasts in a mirror.
Maybe they buried them with my dead poet hands,
in my man's backyard.
I saw angels sitting on his cherry tree last summer.
Some say angels watch the ones you love, for you.
Maybe they were sent because
I could no longer touch him or his lips
and he couldn't find paradise after me.
I wrote poetry to save the both of us from oblivion,
before the words lost their warmth and turned cold.
There is nothing finite about my three sisters;
love, loneliness and grief;
all equally despicable, insufferable and cruel.
There were no suicides,
although the obliteration of our love
hit the headlines.

```
S U R V I V A L
```

No lives were lost
even though something irredeemable
like this world,
died inside.
Once, there was color in all the flowers in the world,
but now, under the burden of this cruel winter
they lie asphyxiated.
And like all the useless bombs in the world
on the cusp of extinction,
my life is layered in silence
and I am just helplessly sitting on it.

- After you, at home in isolation, circa 2020

Sinkhole

I see my mistakes in the mirror every morning,
with a frothy mouth as I aim for a sparkling set of thirty-
two.

It's sad and poetic, how you are everywhere
and my eyes are unforgiving,
now that September was dropped mercilessly
in this sinkhole by you.

My tongue burns and the tap is going to run dry.
I wish I could just have a moment alone.

SURVIVAL

Orgasms

I thought a few seconds of curled toes,
skipped heartbeats, a breath full of stars,
a sigh and a trip to heaven and back,
would end in me being tangled in your arms.

I was so high on love and you,
that I had written myself off, of any possibility
of sleeping alone on the edge of my cold bed
or lying listless on the tiles of my bathroom floor ever
again.

The edge of the bed was for hair falling callously
to the ground,
with your lips scaling every inch of me.
The bathroom tiles were for an impromptu tango,
with our clothes in the audience.

But that was then, and this is now.
Loneliness masquerades as love in my home.
Incorrigibly, I fall deep into its arms
once again and surrender.
But unlike most orgasms that could once shatter the earth,
these are silent, and cry.

SURVIVAL

Poet

And one day,
our poems will speak of our triumphs
more than our brokenness.
And there will be someone,
in the other corner of the world
beyond our years and lifetime,
who will know exactly what it felt like
to be a storm and the calm all at once.
And even if the world doesn't see what we see,
they will know that at least we tried.
We tried over and over again to walk on a minefield and
make it out alive.
Tried being a salve, *where there was pain.*
Tried being a shelter, *where there was rain.*
A voice, *where there were no tongues,*
an embrace, *where there was shame.*
Roses, *where there were guns,*
the light, *where there was no sun.*
We tried and tried and did not quit
and one day hopefully, someone,
will get it.

SURVIVAL

::::

Dahlia

I have dreams, lucid and crystal clear.
I fall to the ground listless.
My bones are slivered like almonds
on the grave of all the tomorrows
that hide a honey glazed story of you and me.
The earth tries to swallow me whole, asphyxiates me.
I am on borrowed time like everything else
that finds a home in its crust.
I will give in and surrender,
but not now, not today.
I am the seed of a blooming dahlia
and in my dreams,
I always make it.

The Remnant

CASS MARIE

ABOUT THE AUTHOR

Cassandra is a creative spirit born and raised in California. She began her writing adventure in her teenage years with short stories, songs, and poetry. Like many others, she needed an outlet for her emotions as she navigated abuse and her own demons, this is where words became a safe haven.

This eventually led to other creative endeavors. Cass now spends her time split between writing, photography and making jewelry.

   @vintage_cass_marie

Naiveté's Echo

I was just a girl
The first time I felt the walls closing in

Too young to understand
But old enough to know it was wrong

Violation being pointed out on a little doll
Black and white text told my story

Yet not a single soul believed me
To this day he still walks this earth freely

I stayed silent
When it happened again at fourteen

Same feeling
Different hands

And you wonder why
Why I chose to close my eyes
Tightly

Shutting out the world around
Pretending this body didn't belong to me

I was just a little girl
When my innocence was stolen

```
SURVIVAL
```

I was just a little girl

Where was my protection?

Scars Omitted

Adolescence was a blur
Arguments and fistfights
My belongings gathered up in trash bags
Self-worth had long ago departed
I viewed myself as walking garbage
Bottled up my emotions
Until I found freedom on the razor's edge
Scabs formed and I'd rip them open
Watch as the pain left through tears in my skin
Took years before anyone even noticed
I was a ghost of the girl I could've been
Therapy came when I showed them
Stepmom writing checks to a woman
who bought the fake smiles
I was a master salesman
"I'm good now, I don't have a problem"
While I tug on my sweater sleeve
So she wouldn't see the fresh cuts
"The medicine is working"
A week later I swallowed all the pills
No one noticed
I was a ghost
They only saw the girl they wanted to see

Where was my advocate?

SURVIVAL

Handle of a Savior

At seventeen I opened my heart
Tore my ribs apart
And let him make a home
Vulnerable and bare
I recalled the trauma, why I'm always on guard
He listened to detailed accounts
Of the bruises that formed when I refused to back down
Promised he was nothing like that
(But alcohol changes people)
It started slowly, so slowly I hardly noted
Soon I was making up excuses
Cleaning up the devastation
Believing the "I'm sorry"
And being shocked when everything shattered
(Again)
I swore I could change him
Stitch him up and heal him
How naive I was
Even knowing what I was up against
Each attempt was nothing but a temporary fix
I gave everything I had to him
And I was left with a hollow chest

Why couldn't I ever be enough?

SURVIVAL

White Lies

A downward spiral as I left
My heart
In pieces stolen by a man with green eyes
And a laugh that could stop me in my tracks
I searched for him
For that feeling
In everyone and everything
Always left more empty

So I traded green eyes for green pills
A new way to reach that high
Found another love in white lines
Avoiding all the signs
Painting myself in lies
Of *"I am just fine"*
Purposely I overlooked
As I let them rummage through
Taking and taking and taking
Only to discard whatever wasn't useful

I thought I knew who I was
But again I was lost
Left
Abandoned
This time by my own hand
If I couldn't count on myself

Who could I trust?

Preemie Premonition

You see,
My life began with a battle
Three months before it was meant to
A tiny heart hooked up to wires
I was born a fighter
There was always something more
A bigger force inside me
Trials and tribulations
Blow after blow
Attempted to make me cower in defeat
I couldn't see it when they took advantage
I tried to kill it with every cut and every pill
I ignored it while green eyes became my obsession
And I found it again when I became clean
Washing my hands while freeing my heart
That little fighter hooked up to wires...
She came back to me
Reminding me
I am my own protector
I am my own advocate
I am enough
It's in that little fighter who defied the odds as they piled up
It's her
It's me
It's that survivor instinct

I can trust

Surviving Suicide

JOE STEELE

ABOUT THE AUTHOR

Joe Steele writes from a place of raw and unfiltered truth. With a wide range of influences such as Edgar Allen Poe, Tupac Shakur and Jim Morrison, his work is driven by the motto 'write without fear', which he prides himself on.

Stemming from his own personal experience with depression and anxiety, which is further evident in his writing, Joe is known for his supportive nature and advocacy for mental health issues.

A highly active member of the Instagram writing community, he has both founded and co-founded four feature pages for which he is both a curator and live host.

In his spare time, Joe enjoys spending time outdoors with his wife Anna and their two children, as well as time at the ice rink with their daughter who figure skates and their son who plays hockey.

 @joesteele401   @Steelepoetry

SURVIVAL

Surviving Suicide

I survived suicidal habits.

Revived,
my mind opened my eyes.
Turned the tides of time.
And now they're on my side.
I've got another chance to fight.
I know it's up to me to grab it,
but I don't have a clue
as to who or what it is
I'm looking for...

Thoughts flood in,
punching me in the throat.
*"SPEAK! Before I fucking destroy
all your hope."*
I stick everything I can
in my ears to stop the noise,
but I struggle to silence
that inner voice.

It fucking kills me
how I can't ever seem to get a break
from the toll it takes on my life,
my body, my kids and my wife.
Every night I lay awake,
consumed by all
my past mistakes.

SURVIVAL

Dwelling on things
that happened before
I was even seventeen.
Still can't seem
to let them go.
They're a part of me,
taunting me worse
than the broken dreams
that haunted my tomorrows.
Every day
I wait for fate
to take me away,
feel like I don't belong–
Impostor Syndrome's
got me barely holding on.

Everything disappears
and you see my blank stares.
Think I don't care,
but I've been in deep,
my own voice weak.
"Please someone,
come rescue me",
I'd beg and plead...
but my cries have
remained unheard.
I was dying there.
How could they sit
and watch me burn?
All it did was reaffirm
that I was right.
That I am just a fucking burden...

SURVIVAL

This isn't something
they taught in class.
Fading fast,
I take one last gasp,
a final attempt.
Extend my arm,
hand outstretched.
Open my eyes
as words fall from the man
who stands in the mirror
before me.

No longer adrift at sea,
my feet find dry land.
Face to face
with my saving grace.
It's him all along,
waiting for me
to finally see
the power I hold,
inside of me.

SURVIVAL

::::

Through Your Pen

It's the same dude,
same shit.
Different names,
same spit.
His game is tight
when he picks these chicks.
He's counting on
their tightened lips.
That's the game.
It only works one way.
A lone wolf
who loves to play.
Hides in the shadows
in the light of day.
But when darkness looms,
his confidence blooms.
He speaks in tongues.
Jaded, you can't see the truth.
You hear his entrancing lines.
His jowls become tense.
He growls,
still you hear poetic rhymes.
Suddenly you feel the suspense.
The moon appears,
he howls out.
His rage has you bleeding from the mouth.
Finally, you see who he really is.
Scared and hurt,
you start to scream and shout.

SURVIVAL

But no one hears your desperate cries.
When it's over and he finally sets you free,
you speak your truth,
but it seems as if no one believes in you.
You run and hide,
you're contemplating suicide.
You remember what happened the last time you tried.
But this time you think it through.
Learned from past mistakes.
No more pills, no more blades.
"This time I'll get a gun."
In hope you'll finally feel numb.
You pull the trigger.
The gun slips.
Grazes your scalp.
Concussion hits.
Out cold on the floor.
Mom comes flying through the door.
Frantically dials.
She thinks you're dead.
The blood drips,
carpet soaked in red.
You come to,
and realize that you survived once again.
You thought you had no friends.
But one woman refused to let this be the end.
She knew your pain.
She saw the trend.
Her own suicide attempt flashed in her head.
She called 911.
Knowing, you were not yet done.
Now you thrive through your pen.
Telling your story until who knows when.

SURVIVAL

:::

Stubborn

I don't write poetry for the masses,
I write poetry to raise glasses.
A toast to those
who know what it's like
to feel emotions so strong
they part oceans.
When I write my thoughts and feelings,
they always have a rhyme
or a reason.
A purpose for every time or season.
I hope to shine a light for those who only see darkness,
to keep them believing.
Sometimes it's on the surface,
but there's always a deeper meaning.

In truth,
I've inked the eyes of my mind with pen to paper.
Never meant
to be sublime or stiff neck.
I'm just a guy from white trash wastelands,
trying to make the best
of the iniquitous mess.
Mashed up inside,
this sentenced sinner's head.
I love you all more than I'll ever love myself.
I've placed guns to my temple,
only wanting one thing.
To be an example to others of what not to do,
but I realize actions speak louder than words.

SURVIVAL

And so I live on with these untold burdens.
I'll soak up my pain and keep on hurting.
I never wanted to be a statistic,
don't want my mom to ever know
what it's like to pull ballistics.
To have to identify an empty shell of what once was.
She is the sun,
and I, the earth.
And since she gave birth,
I have no right to decide when it's my time.
I just sit and contemplate the caverns of life's tragedies.
And I wonder what it is,
that's really stopping me.
I guess I'm stubborn to the point of no return.
Willing to watch myself burn.

When will I learn?
I am not the opponent in my life's story.
I am player one.
And I've been lucky to re-up my life more than once.
Because I know what it's like,
to have guns placed in places that distort faces and
rearrange teeth.
Leaving little to no traces of who it is beneath those clean
white sheets.
Lying in stains of blood,
leaving nothing left.
No life, empty veins,
and barely any brains.
A tragedy worse
than standing in front of trains until the last second.

SURVIVAL

I had no choice,
because when I played chicken,
it was my friend Lenny who got scared.
He saved a boy
whose brain was impaired.
A lost boy who didn't know any better
than to not be scared.
I know I went off track,
so let's get back to why and how I write-
I write how I lived,
and now I live to write.

Sleepwalking

The silence was deafening-
I never knew what that meant.
Until one night,
I was lost in the woods
with nothing, not even a tent.
Faced with survival,
and trying to find my bearings.
I started out angry,
throwing sticks and swearing.
Then it occurred to me
that this wasn't the answer.
I had a choice to make,
and the choice
couldn't have been clearer.
To stay calm and succeed
in the face of hard times.
I would have to remain focused
if I wanted to make it out alive.
When the silence began to subside,
the noise struck fear in the back of my mind.
The crunch of the leaves
underneath my feet,
the breaking of sticks
from the tops of the trees.
No one to help-
it was all on me.
I pinched and poked,
grabbed and groped,
but it was all just hope,

SURVIVAL

hope that it was all just a dream.
But this was reality,
a nightmare of a scene.
What dangers lie in wait?
I had to stay still and silent
while I stayed awake.
To make a noise,
any at all,
would invite the predators in,
and surely I'd fall.
And these minutes felt like hours,
time passed so slow,
then all at once, daylight
began to show.
And now the journey
is set to begin.
To be in my home,
was my only wish.
This would be a walk to remember,
in this blistering cold month of November.
Then off in the distance,
a familiar sight hit my eyes.
It was my home,
much to my surprise.
I couldn't believe
it was so close,
but I was grateful,
because I tend
to sleepwalk without clothes.
Just me, baring my soul.

Live

I'm tired, tired of being.
The others, they laugh at me.
Tell me I'm nothing,
and I believe them.
I was going to prove them right.
That was my plan,
then I gave up
I had no fight
Nothing left, no desire.
No will.
Just emptiness,
and a bottle.
Nope, not pills.
That's not my style.
Something sweeter.
Southern Comfort.
And a twelve pack, just in case.
Drown my sorrows in sorrow.
Just hoping I wouldn't
see tomorrow.
But that day always came.
It became a game.
One I'd lose every time
my eyes were awakened.
Back then, time seemed stagnant.
Everything was a blur.
I was done with life,
I'd just had it, I had no worth.
I saw no value living in this place.
I wasn't worthy of the space.

SURVIVAL

And I couldn't be forgiven.
I had buried myself years before,
only to resurrect the demons inside.
I missed them, they never lied.
There's a certain beauty,
in that kind of truth.
I know because I'm the living proof.
I'm writing out here.
And they are locked,
locked inside a tiny booth.
It's all on me.
If they come out,
it's something I choose.
I turned the game.
Flipped the script.
Turned them into my muse,
and I know
they'll never control me again.
But that doesn't mean
we won't dance
around the darkest recesses
of my head.
I have no choice
but to continue on,
I have to.
I've got too much shit
I still haven't said.
I want to live, until I'm dead.

One, Two, Three, Four
I Declare a Survival War

K.M. LENNAN

ABOUT THE AUTHOR

K.M. Lennan is a writer and poet grown from the intricate roots of her small town, American Midwest upbringing.

Writing provided a means of survival and growth through all the challenging seasons of her life, from a young age on. Words have not only saved her countless times, but have given her the space to bloom.

Her words can be found on Instagram under the handle @inktswords.

   @inktswords   inktswords

Haunted, Have You Ever

Have you ever been haunted?

Really, truly, haunted...

Where nightmares are a welcomed breath of fresh air because they save you from reality?

I have.

Where every step you take sounds like a stampeding crowd is chasing you, even though you know you're all alone?

I have.

Where endless voices scream without mercy or tire, repeating the same cycle of words (that you could never stomach the first time), like a broken, skipping record that you can never turn off?

I have.

Have you ever heard a sound so loud, so piercing, it felt like a million shards of glass sliced into your eardrums, embedded themselves and made a home?

I have.

Have you ever seen something so frightening, your skin turned itself inside out and crawled inside your bones?

SURVIVAL

I have.

Have you ever opened up your eyes, only to find the world has been engulfed by giant tsunami waves striking over and over again?

I have.

Have you ever struggled so hard to breathe you actually had to reach out and grab for handfuls of air, then race to stuff it down your throat, into your lungs, before it slipped through your fingers?

I have.

Have you ever looked at someone who you knew inside and out, someone you loved with all you had, someone you would have given your own life for, and watched their face melt off, right before your eyes, because it was never their face at all?

I have.

Have you ever lost an entire circle of friends you considered to be family, because they didn't believe that you didn't know?

I have.

Have you ever curled up in bed, completely clothed and alone, only to wake up naked and in the presence of someone you thought was your friend?

SURVIVAL

I have.

Have you ever told your other friends what happened to you in that bedroom and had them question your story, despite the proof of your torn clothing and fingerprint bruises... All because he said you weren't unconscious and didn't say no?

I have.

Have you ever had a friend hand-deliver letters from the man who raped you, because he said he loved you and wanted you to come visit him in prison?

I have.

Have you ever asked your friend how she could still support a man who's been imprisoned twice for sexual crimes that occurred AFTER he got away with raping you? Only to have her look you in the eyes and say...

"He says he didn't do any of those things and I just don't know what to believe."?

I have.

Have you ever felt like you were standing in front of an open crowd, jumping up and down, waving frantically, and everyone was looking right through you?

I have.

Have you ever felt like you were screaming louder than you've ever screamed anything in your entire life, but no

SURVIVAL

one could hear you because someone else kept hitting the mute button?

I have.

Have you ever lived inside a tiny snow globe, dancing along blissfully to the music in the clouds, only to have someone drop your entire world and let it shatter into a billion pieces on the ground?

I have.

Have you ever had the people who claimed to love you and know you best tell you that they don't know how to handle a broken you, and instead of trying to figure it out, they just disappear and leave you alone to drown?

I have.

Have you ever secretly known the reason they all left is because they didn't believe you?

I have.

Have you ever been so traumatized by a person's actions that even eight years later, you still can't say what he did aloud?

I have.

I am.

{But I'm almost there.}

SURVIVAL

Have you ever always been the strong one and suddenly found yourself floating in an unknown universe where people use words like "victim", "abuse", and "survivor"?

I have.

Have you ever tried to find the words to help others who haven't been there themselves get just the tiniest glimpse into how it feels?

I have.

I just did.

SURVIVAL

Earth, Vapor, Fingers

I can feel it coming
Like the beating of a drum
Though my eyes are wandering,
They are fixed
And locked
And honed

The earth is hard
Yet my feet sink
The heaviness of each step growing
Closing…
Closing
Can I reach?

How did we get here?

It's just you and me
I only tried to love you
I tried to let you love me
Now I can't breathe

I can't breathe

The earth is hard
The earth is hard and the air is hot around me
The earth is hard, the air is hot,
And I am running.
I am running for my life
My life

SURVIVAL

I only need to reach the door

The earth is hard
The earth is hard, and I am running
The earth is hard, and I am running
For the door
Your breath is loud behind me
I can feel you breathe,
I can feel you reaching
I can feel you

I can feel you breathe

The earth is hard
The earth is hard, the air is hot
The earth is hard, the air is hot,
Your breath is loud
The earth is hard, the air is hot,
Your breath is loud,
And your fingers burn
As they grab me

I can feel you breathe

The earth is hard
The earth is hard and my feet tumble
I can feel you breathe
Your breath is loud, the air is hot
The earth is hard
The earth is spinning

I can feel you breathe

SURVIVAL

The earth is gone
The earth is gone, my feet can't find it
The earth is gone, my feet can't find it,
But I can feel the blow to the back of my head
I can feel the blow
To the back of my head
As you lift me
I can feel the blow to the back of my head
As you lift me from the ground

I can feel you breathe

I can feel you breathe
I can feel you breathe, but I can't
I can't breathe myself

I can't breathe

How did we get here?

It's just you and me
I only tried to love you
I tried to let you love me
Now I can't breathe

I can't breathe

Your eyes stare back at me
Caverns of earth coveting a lost soul
All I can see is your eyes

Your eyes

SURVIVAL

Your hands are tight
Your hands are tight on my throat
Your hands are tight on my throat
And I can feel you breathe
As you press
But I can't
I can't breathe,
But you can

Your eyes
Your eyes stare back at me
Cold and calculating
Bold and evaluating
Your hands are tight
And I'm fighting

I am fighting.

Your hands are tight
And I am fighting for my life
Your eyes
Your hands

I can feel you breathe, but I can't

The earth is gone
The world is gone
All I can see is you
All I can feel is you
Your breath
Your eyes
Your hands
My life

SURVIVAL

How did we get here?

It's just you and me
I only tried to love you
I tried to let you love me
Now I can't breathe

I can't breathe

Your eyes
I can't feel anything
I can't see anything
But your eyes
Your eyes
Your hands are clasped
I can feel you breathe

I can feel you breathe, but I can't

Your face is fading
Your face is fading but your eyes
I can reach your eyes
Your hands are tight
Your hands are tight and I am fighting

I am fighting

Your hands are tight and I am fighting
For my life
Your eyes
I can feel you breathe
I can feel you breathe and I can hear you scream
Your eyes

SURVIVAL

I can hear you scream
As I fight for my life

Your eyes

Your hands are tight
Your hands are tight and I am weak
Your hands are tight and I am weak
But I can reach
Your eyes
And I fight
I fight to breathe

I fight to breathe

The earth is hard
The earth is hard and it hurts
The earth is hard and it hurts
As I'm crashing
Surrounded by blinding light
The earth is hard and it hurts
As I'm crashing
And I don't even care
Because I can breathe
I can breathe

I can breathe

I hear the other voices
I hear the other voices
And I can feel the earth
I hear the other voices
And I can feel the earth

SURVIVAL

And I can finally breathe

How did we get here?

It was just you and me
You wouldn't let me go
You wouldn't let me breathe
I only tried to love you
I tried to let you love me

The earth is hard
The earth is hard
But I don't even care because…

I can breathe.

Hide and Seek

All the world's a game, of
"Ready or not, here I come!"

And I'm never ready
I'm never, ever ready
But they always, always come
They always come for me

Hide and Seek

Tear me down
Build me up
Hunker down
Rise above

Hands seeking...

Sometimes they're theirs
Sometimes they're mine

Bodies hiding...

Sometimes it's theirs
Sometimes it's mine

Secrets keeping...

Sometimes they're theirs
Sometimes they're mine

SURVIVAL

Endless counting...

Minutes 'til I see you
Breaths since I've cried

Hide and Seek

The slate is clean

I seek to find

Danger is near

I seek to hide

Brick by brick
They throw, and I build
Back and forth
To kill or be killed

Hide and Seek

One, two,
Life is coming for you
Three, four,
It will break down your door
Five, six,
Build your wall high with bricks
Seven, eight,
Watch out - danger awaits
Nine, ten,
Never sleep again

SURVIVAL

Hide and Seek

How strong is strong?
How weak is weak?
What's the threshold for catastrophe?
How many losses until they count
as a streak?

Hide and Seek

Extra! Extra! Read all about it!
This week I'm strong
Next week, I'm doubting

Hide and Seek

Fighting the ghosts
To keep them contained
Burying loved ones
In freshly dug graves

Hide and Seek

Seek me, and love me
But "love me" too much
Chronic Stalk Me Syndrome
You think you own my touch

Hide and Seek

Hands of unwanted advance
Repeat throughout life

SURVIVAL

Robbed of my voice
Since I was a child

Hide and Seek

'Til death do us part
Words of love between
Husband and wife
Never meant for them to mean
I'd have to fight for my life

Hide and Seek

I bend and I blend
I cover and protect
Little by little
I lose myself

Hide and Seek

I rarely win,
But I always ***survive.***

Fortress

I know everything there is to know
About one sided,
Unrequited
Love...
But absolutely nothing about
Being loved equally
In return
I wish there was someone else
Who I could blame for this,
But there isn't
No, this one...
This one, is on me

Someone once said
That sometimes…
"People build walls,
Not to keep people out,
But to see who cares enough
To knock them down."
But if you know me
You know
I don't want mine torn down
I absolutely build them
To keep people out
To keep me in
To keep me safe

SURVIVAL

I've got walls you can see
Walls you cannot
Walls you can't climb
Overgrown with poisonous vines
Walls within walls
Built up carefully
Brick by brick
Reinforced with concrete
Then reinforced again with steel
So they're slick

I dug a moat outside
Filled it with creatures of fright
Every mythical fire-breathing dragon
I could find
Alligators and crocodiles, alike
Sharpen their teeth every day
Piranhas, for the swimmers of brave
Replaced the water with gasoline
One flick of a match would ignite
I'm in this castle for solitude
In this cave to stay alive

I do not wish to be found…
Inside my dungeon,
I am free
I am me
I am darkness
I am light
I am a fading silence
Whispering in the night

SURVIVAL

I am empty
I am whole
I am broken
Without control
I am somber
I am weak
I am hope abstained
From the answers I seek

In the shadows, I may break
But that is okay,
Because this is MY place
In here I am sheltered
From the claws of emotion
From the hands of the wanting
The nails of the needing
The knife of the knowing
Cut myself open
Bleed out the words I couldn't say
Funnel my thoughts into jars
Piss out my hopes
Shit out my dreams
Flush them all away
Like they never haunted me at all

Peel my skin off
And hang it up for the night
Bury my bones in the dirt
Sprinkle on some wishes like fertilizer
Hoping that I'll grow…
Spread that around, and water it

```
SURVIVAL
```

Light a candle
Hum a spell
Make an offering
I don't have much to give,
But I give it
I give it all
I give it so much
There is nothing left of me

I'm a shell
I'm a ghost
A glimpse
A glimmer
That shadow you see
Out of the corner of your eye
But when you turn
There is nothing
Nothing there
Nothing here
Nothing to see
Nothing anywhere
How could there be?

There are no windows
No cracks in the wall
To let the light trickle in
No doors
No secret hidden entryways
You cannot come here
You were not invited
And you are not welcome

SURVIVAL

Not in my fortress
Not in me

I see you looking
See you reading
See your wheels turning
As you think you are beginning
To see
To know
To understand something
Anything about me
Those pieces I gave
And gave
And gave to you
I take
I take them
I take them back
I take them all back
One by one, they disappear
Gone, like they never existed at all

I pick them up
Fill my arms with the pieces of me
I sprinkled all around
Toss them into a pile
With the rest of my junk
Douse them with fluid
And strike a match
Let the flames swallow them whole
Like they never existed
They never were

SURVIVAL

Burning embers of my love
And my laughter
Scorching my pain
And my disaster
Engulfing the desires
That brought me life
Exploding like the volcano that I am
I lay in the lava and swim
Back floating across my dark night
Cascading my silence away from the light

And then,

I Say Goodnight.

Olly Olly Oxen Free

I dreamed a dream
I dreamed a life
I fought the world
I sacrificed
I bent my will
I paid a price
I adapted to change
I evolved to survive
The world was heavy
But I carried it strong
Filing away every burden
Because it didn't belong
And I lived…
Despite the darkness inside my walls
I lived

I was a warrior in my fortress and I was strong
Because I survived
And I was untouchable
I had found the secret to protecting myself from the dangers Of the world
I was safe…
I was alive
I was safe
And I told myself that separation was survival

But I wasn't surviving
I was dying

```
SURVIVAL
```

I was suffocating in my own grave
Surrounded by people who didn't love me
Because I didn't let them know me
I was too afraid
Drowning myself in the tears
I refused to allow myself to cry
Swimming in the lakes of forgotten wants
Because I stopped asking why

All I had were memories,
I wasn't making any new
My process of survival was killing me
Existing isn't living
Just because I was alive,
Didn't mean I was alright
There's a difference between surviving and being okay
I wasn't okay
And in this case….
It wasn't okay not to be okay

I needed to burn
Ashes, ashes, we all fall down
And down, I fell
Crashing
Crashing and cracking
Until I was bleeding open and wide
Upon my self-built altar
I rectified
Piece by piece
Pain by pain
Every haunting ghost I tried to erase
Every memory I couldn't face

SURVIVAL

A journey through time
Relived in my mind
Words as my weapons
Burning each grave as I dug out its bones
No longer afraid
I would rise and I'd grow
Facing my demons
So I could destroy them
Burn them
Survive them
Survive my survival

Reignite
The fire that always should have burnt within
The fire that I forgot to tend to
The flame that was buried in pain
Because I forgot
I forgot about the spark
Or maybe
Maybe I was just afraid
Afraid to light it
Because I had been burnt
Too many times before
But see... that's the thing about fire
It doesn't really burn you
If you hold it just right
Let it grow
Let it warm you
Let it shield you from the cold
Burn away everything that's dead
All around you
Leave room for new life

SURVIVAL

So what say you?
Are you dead?
Or are you breathing?
And if you're breathing,
Are you living?
Or just surviving?

Olly olly oxen free...

Bare Bones

DENA HELMER

ABOUT THE AUTHOR

Born and raised in Central Illinois, Dena, the sibling of three brothers, one sister, and the single mother of two beautiful girls, was drawn to writing at a young age. Always slinging verbiage and doodling thoughts in a thin, red notebook, she wrote her first rhyme at the age of eight.

Life happened as it does, from that moment until the now, but she's getting back to her heart's passion. Dena stumbled onto the Instagram scene in 2015. After building confidence, she shared her pieces, little by little, which allowed a crossing of paths with Carlos Medina, as well as, countless other talented writers.

She hopes to inspire, provoke, and draw others in, with her words. After all, we all have stories to tell. Some of us just need to know we aren't alone, to share our own. Fear can keep our voices silenced, if we allow it. Don't let it silence yours.
As the quote below describes, if you think things are impossible, she will show you why anything IS possible.

Her words, something she stands by -

"Never think the possible, is impossible."

 @dena_80   denanay80

Interpretation of Reflection

I have scars. More than enough on my face, but I can point out three right now that I don't necessarily always smile at.

One in my eyebrow, from my head being hit against something, or being hit in the head. More than likely, both. One on my cheekbone, from being hit with a fist. That alone, occurred enough to last 10 lifetimes. One in my dimple... a knife. A shiny, somewhat dull, steak knife.

I remember being scared, his hand groping my face. My body shaking. The fear in me, damn near making me pass out. Yet, I couldn't move. I couldn't do a damn thing to stop whatever he was planning on doing.

That one memory of a thousand that still gets triggered, if anyone near me holds a knife.

I have internal struggles, due to the detailed aspects pertaining to that memory and the unforgotten past. I am constantly working on me. Gaining strength. Becoming who I have always been, who I knew I could always be, before I was broken and beaten down, repeatedly... in the literal sense.

These things, all the reminders of way back when, I don't always like about myself. I reflect a lot. I question myself. Not out of fear or missing the 'used to be' things, but to overcome, even if I feel like I've already kicked the past's ass.

SURVIVAL

I can't change these things. And to be honest, I don't think I would if I could. But what's even more important, is these things happening to me, DIDN'T change me.

It didn't change my heart. It didn't change my mindset, in a negative way at least. It didn't alter the human in me. The good parts. If anything, it all molded them. It lined dull parts of me with gold.

And though I don't always like these things about myself, I have accepted them. I have embraced them. They don't make me hide away. They don't make me hate myself. I have more love for myself now, than I think I ever have. I'm forever evolving into something and someone I WANT to be. Not who I am supposed to be, or expected to be. I'm me. And that's fucking amazingly beautiful. ONWARD AND UPWARD. OVERCOMING AND EXCELLING.

My girls, my reasons, they need to know that ALL is possible. They need to believe it. And if they don't already, they will. I'll make sure of it.

That's what I'm here for...

Missing Piece

I didn't find out until after the fact. I didn't know until it was too late. She didn't make it. She was gone. She died on the operating table. I learned this, via text message. She died. *She fucking died.* And I was frozen inside.

Physically, my body reacted. I flung the Keurig across the room. I beat the living shit out of an uncaring countertop. I screamed. I fell to my knees, trying to understand the 'whys'. The 'hows'. The 'what the fucks'. I didn't understand it. My Mom, the woman who birthed me, whom I hadn't seen or spoken to since the summer of 2008, had lost her life at the age of fifty-seven. *Fifty-seven.*

2014 was here, and she was gone. No chance of hearing her voice again. No chance of ever laying my eyes upon her again. No chance of getting the hug that only a mom knows how to give. No chance of ever telling her, "I'm sorry".

You see, I made a choice in 2008. I was given an ultimatum. It was either my mom, or my family. My girls' dad, he bestowed this wonderful choice on me, or else. So a choice was made. I chose my family out of fear. Fucking fear. Nevermind that I thought I'd always have my mom. I mean, who loses their mom at such a young age? Well, I did. I was thirty-three. And yes, I had gone years without "needing" her. But, inside, I never stopped needing her. She was my mom.

SURVIVAL

She wasn't always the easiest to love, but I loved her that much harder. Not because I had to, but because she needed me to.

The guilt that is carried, is deep and wide. I have learned that I cannot change the past, however, I cannot let go of chances passed.

I miss her. I am still going on with my life, because that's what I'm supposed to do. That's what she would want. Being the best mom for my girls, is my own mom's legacy. And I can only hope the choices I have made, and continue to make, fill her with pride.

I feel her near sometimes. The scent of her perfume. When it hits me, I'm at a complete standstill. It consumes me. I close my eyes and take in every breath of that scent I can, until it has dissipated. I know she's close. I sense it. She has a way of letting me know she's around. Songs play. Goosebumps ensue. And tears, well, they don't make it all the way down my cheeks, before they are wiped away. I can't explain it. But, it keeps me going.

I know she forgives me for the choice I made. I know she loves me. I know that because, when I went to the hospital the day after she passed away, the nurse who took care of her came over to me. There were ten people standing around. I wasn't the only female, but she came to me. And she said, "You must be Dena." I nodded my head yes with slight hesitation, and she proceeded to tell me what my mom wanted me to know. I clung to every single word.

Along with guilt, I carry that knowledge. I carry that love. I carry those words that she wanted me to hear. She gives me all the strength, even at my weakest.

I carry her, in my heart, always. She's where she belongs...

⋮

Beginning of an End

4:30am. Seems so early, after not getting to sleep till 1:30, and after working 17 hours. But again, my body is used to being up at 5am for work. This day though, this day, was my day off. Instead of sleeping in, I was awakened by pain. A crippling pain in my stomach. It was happening. Shit! What I knew to be inevitable, was finally coming to fruition.

You see, just a few short weeks before this, I had gone to the doctor, after taking five pregnancy tests. Five pregnancy tests that all revealed the same.... positive. *How is this possible? What the fuck am I going to do now?* I didn't want this. I protected myself, at all costs. The relationship I was in was not a healthy one, and to be honest, I knew it was over long before quits was called. I had no business being in one. Do I even want to accredit him by speaking about this now? No. Hell fucking no. However, it happened.

As selfish as it sounds, I didn't want any more children. I had my girls, and my heart was full. I was creating a life for us, and weeding out the shit that brought me down, as well as healing from an abusive marriage. Now this??

SURVIVAL

I prayed a lot. I prayed to God. Why would He do this, knowing I've already lost so much? Why would He do this, knowing I don't want more? Why would He give me something that others yearn to have? The fairness, it just wasn't there.

My doctor's appointment revealed that I was nine weeks. Nine weeks, but only measuring six weeks, per ultrasound.

That discovery led to the words I was expecting to hear, "We can't find a heartbeat, Dena."

After examining internally, just to ensure what she had said was correct, it was decided that I would come back in a week.

Maybe they just couldn't find it. Maybe it was too early. Maybe it was something else.

Either way, I was going to that appointment in a week. Bottom line, my first appointment was set to begin with, so I could talk of my options. My heart was broken, knowing I had to make a decision, whatever that was. Torn. Selfishly torn. I'm not built to hurt others. I'm not built to destroy life. I'm not built for denying gifts and blessings, regardless of any situation.

But I was. In my head and in my heart, I was doing all of that.

Fast forward a week... a week of wondering. A week of constant praying, cussing, asking the same questions.... "*Why? How? What the? Seriously?*" The follow-up appointment confirmed the prior week's news. No heartbeat.

SURVIVAL

Now, at this point, I was saddened. Saddened beyond what my mind could comprehend. Saddened this was the end of a beginning. Sad that a living, breathing being was inside of me, and nothing I could do was going to save it.

Sad, for so many reasons.

If I said I wasn't relieved that I didn't have to make a choice, I'd be straight fucking lying to you. Truth is though, I was. I honestly didn't know how I was supposed to feel about that moment.

Numbness took over. The reality of what was to come hadn't quite hit me yet. But I knew it was coming.

Three days later, my relationship ended, by his own actions. I never told him I had taken tests, or that I had gone to the doctor. Was that wrong of me? Maybe, but this, was not a reason to stay in that level of toxicity.

4:30am came with a vengeance. I was alone. Crying.

I could barely walk from my bedroom to the bathroom. My God, the pain. I ran some bath water. I figured the best thing I could do, would be to sit in that tub. Cry in that tub. I wish I could tell you how many times in that moment that I wished it wasn't happening. I lost count. I felt incredible guilt. Tremendous guilt. The blaming of myself... *I caused this, right?* For two hours, I sat in that tub, going through the process of losing an unborn baby. Feeling it. Seeing it. In disbelief of it.

SURVIVAL

I believe, wholeheartedly, that everything happens for a reason. EVERYTHING. I wasn't prepared for that kind of mental wraparound, but, I believe I needed it. A strength stemmed from that day. A strength I never knew I had, nor needed. I believe that it happened the way it did, so that I didn't have to make that decision.

God gave me something, knowing how it was going to end, knowing my stance on it, to wake me up in a sense. I don't know any other way to look at it. I prayed for answers. I prayed for strength to guide a choice, before I knew I didn't even have

to make one. When it was happening, and after the fact, I prayed for the strength to help me through it all. Strength to forgive myself for the thoughts that went through my head. Strength to accept that I'm only human. And in my heart, though I struggled with what I didn't want at that time, I turned to who I needed. And He came through.

Today, I am stronger in every aspect. And I know for certain, I was given everything I didn't know I needed that day. In every single way possible.

A realization of unforeseen blessings...

Lost Circumstance

The cool thing to do, so I heard. Everyone was doing it. Well, everyone but me. Sixteen. Sixteen, young, naïve, but smart. Smart enough to know what I didn't want to do, and who I didn't want to be. I didn't want to be like my friends. I was a good girl... the innocent one. The one who didn't drink or do drugs. The one who was there for everyone else. But I was also the ugly friend. The fat freckle-faced friend. The friend who didn't have boys gawking at her... who didn't get the attention friends got. Though that probably hurt a bit, it didn't make me turn into the slutty girl. The attention-seeking girl. I was always just, me.

Sixteen and living at my dad's house with my oldest brother, who's six years older than me... a drinker. Obnoxious. It's who he's always been, and still, who he is now.

My best friend was over for the night. We made plans earlier in the week to have a sleepover and eat junk food. Why not? My best friend... my brother thought she was the hottest thing since, I don't know, Mac n Cheese? He thought all my friends were hot. And they were beautiful.

It was winter. A fire was occupying the fireplace. There was a knock on the door. A friend of my brother's arrived. Apparently, they had planned on drinking. Great... so much for hanging out with my friend, watching movies and being a fat kid. How annoying.

As the night went on, alcohol was consumed. My brother and his friend, they were pretty buzzed, I'm certain of it.

SURVIVAL

My brother, all over my friend. Again, how annoying. I was sitting on the far side of the couch, when my brother's friend decided to come sit next to me. Like, why? And ummmm, no! I couldn't sit there anymore. I wasn't comfortable. It was awkward, and well, I wasn't going to stay in that space. At that point, I let my bestie know I was going to bed and went to my room.

My bed, a white metal daybed. Hunter green sheets (my favorite color at the time) and a matching comforter, waited for me. I laid down and turned to face the wall. A short time later, I heard my door open. I was too tired to turn over to see who it was, assuming it was my friend anyway. I said, "Your bed is ready for you, C." (I had made the trundle bed up for her a bit earlier.)

Next thing I knew, someone was on top of me. Hand over my mouth. My heart, beating out of my chest. I couldn't see anything. It was dark. So fucking dark. I tried to move, or at least I thought I did. I was frozen. Paralyzed. All but my arms were moving to get myself out of there. But the weight of him... he used it all.

He was so heavy, I felt like I was a piece of paper trapped under a boulder. A hand pushed my shorts down. The other hand, still on my mouth. I heard a zipper. Screams tore through my head, *"What the fuck is going on here? I'm dreaming. Yes... I'm dreaming. Fuck, Dena... wake up!"*

He took his pants off. I felt my arms restrained with one hand, and the other, still on my mouth. I tried to kick and move my legs. His weight was too much for me to budge. And then, the moment I knew for certain I wasn't in a dream. I was in a living nightmare.

I felt it. I couldn't stop it. I couldn't scream loud enough. I couldn't help myself. I couldn't stop him from taking what was mine... my innocence. It was gone. Stolen. Fucking taken!

I didn't feel wanted. I surely didn't feel needed. I felt dirty. Used. Disgusting. Pathetic. Whatever worth I thought I had at that moment, disintegrated into that stifling air.

When it was over, the nightmare didn't end. I couldn't sleep. I couldn't move. I couldn't breathe. I couldn't wrap my young mind around what had just happened. I couldn't speak. I was numb, yet in so much pain. *What did I do to cause this?* A question I asked myself more times than I can count. I never once slept in that bed again. Blood painted the white metal now. My beautiful sheets and comforter, tainted in every way. It wasn't my bed anymore.

I never spoke of this until years later. I was ashamed. Embarrassed. Self-blaming in ways that were detrimental to my mindset. And to be honest, only less than a handful of people knew, until now.

No, I will never get back what was taken. I can't change that it happened. I can't wish the memory away. I CAN however, learn from it, grow from it, and break the cycle of that act alone, dictating how the rest of my life is lived. There are positives in it. A strength that arose. It took me a long time to find it, but I did. Letting go of a fault I placed upon myself was the biggest release. Strength. It didn't kill me, though I wanted to die. Strength. It didn't define me, I define me. Strength. And my worth, it's intact. I find that, and define that, within myself.

Don't let the happenings of your life paint a picture of who you are meant to be. Only you can define you.

SURVIVAL

Define without judgement of yourself. And get out of the fucking mindset of, "Nothing good ever happens to me", or, "I guess I'm just meant to have a shitty life."

Yes, it does.

And no, you're not.

Shit happens to the best of us. Daily. Unexpectedly. You have the power within, to change life as you know it. Don't wait. Engage your worth. You have to want it bad enough.

Want it, and make it so...

The Tough Call

"Fear: an unpleasant emotion caused by the belief that someone or something is dangerous, likely to cause pain, or a threat."
- Dictionary definition: Oxford Languages

We all know this as the definition of fear. I have let that word define life for me, more than I care to admit. Let's be honest, we all have. Which is probably why you chose to pick this book up, and read the words within the pages.

Fear, it stifles us. It leaves us stagnant. It silences our voices. It shames our beliefs. It consumes every part of who we are and dictates all the moves we cannot make. It deters us from the choices we want to make. And in all honesty, the ones we should make. Fear is what makes us afraid of the tomorrows after today. It's what keeps the drinks in our hands, the pills in our pockets, the needles in our arms, and the negative mindset that things will never get better. It's what takes dreams, and creates nightmares. It's what feels right, because we are used to the Hell it keeps us in. Knowing anything else is foreign.

So why budge from the familiar? Comfort goes hand in hand with fear. Comfort's biggest enemy is courage. Courage. We all know the definition of courage, right? If you don't, Google it. After you do that, read it. Read it again. And then again. Embed it in your head.

The more pressure you put on fear, the weaker it becomes.

When you inform yourself, strength arises. When strength arises, steps are taken. When steps are taken, paths are paved. When paths are paved, fear can most definitely be left behind.

SURVIVAL

Make the choice. Make the fucking choice to fight against the fear that you hold within. Make the choice to live the life you were given. No, nothing is easy. Life isn't easy. It's not even close to being fucking easy. It's not supposed to be. But God damn it, you're a warrior! And warriors, they power through and overcome.

Take the leap. Relinquish control. Let's be honest, you don't have it anyway, fear does. Fear isn't the final act. It's not the end scene of a predictable movie. It's a feeling. An emotion. Shake it. Strangle it. Exhaust it. Do everything you can to rid yourself of it, but never feed it. The more you feed it, the greater it becomes. Starve it. Fuel what lies in your heart and in your soul.

No act is ever final. There's always an encore, right? When you walk off that stage, don't turn around and look. Don't take the bow. Give one last, "Fuck you", to fear, and move on. Just like when you feel trapped in a bad relationship, there's a way out. I assure you there is. There's a way around it. There is freedom from walking away from all that has worked to keep you small. Fuck that. Be free. Know it's possible. I promise you it is, and every struggle will be worth it. I know, I'm proof of that.

I regret nothing. I know there is light after the darkest night. I know because I didn't stop until I found it. And now, I refuse to live in the shadows of fear. Any shadows. I live. Because living is better than dying any slow death dictated by someone, or something else. Choose to live. Choose to know that you are worth more than any fear's wrath.

You're a SURVIVOR. You're still here, aren't you?

You have worth. Believe it. Believe in you...

Tadasana

ALEX LE'GARE

ABOUT THE AUTHOR

Having found a true knack for literature as a child, Alex Le'Gare has prided himself on delivering rhyme, rhythm, and introspection via poetry for virtually his entire life. He credits his willingness to be open-minded and the fact that he is a recluse by nature, to his undying love and motivation for creative writing. His only goal is to inspire others to create and be as free as he is through not only the mind, but the pen.

His debut poetry collection "The Side Effects of L" is available now on Amazon.

 @alex.legare

Sleeves

Let's meet in the smoke
Hold hands and wave at the haze
Stand our ground and rise above
Lock your eyes with mine
So that you're not too hard to find
Fleeing from the front line
Should I lose you
Move your mask from your mouth
Tell me where you are
Scream from where's seemingly safe
I'll bring strength
On a mission, not to miss you
Take cover
I've got sleeves to help you leave
Grab my arms and wish for wings
After all
They're shooting at us

SURVIVAL

::::

Yesterday's Storms

Quiet as a prayer in public
Too busy watching what everyone worships
Hesitation heeds
What else is there--
to believe?
Trust me
I'm fine
Pruned and wrinkled by an overzealous sky
Yesterday's storms
Baptized me / on the back end
With my eyes by the hilt
I saw everything go
My eyelids are for show
They don't work unless they're wide
Like a witness to whatever went away
With an ability to see it twice
And not ever miss a thing

Interlude

Those flags we picked up
were fully stained
pale ones

Blotched
with the blood
from the battles
that built us

Next to the weapons
that never killed us

Our clothes
look like we've stepped on a landmine

We can't feel
our legs

But it's nice to meet you

SURVIVAL

Shade

Strangers love
You don't know me
I'm not from around here
I came from out of trees
With glass for leaves
Each autumn -- drips my shrapnel
Strips my shade
Spiraling down toward a stay
Reflecting on grounds
Where I'm resting my roots

Tadasana

Touched by ecru through lilac veins
You'd think that heartbeat broke glass
That marteau -- made whole;
on yoga mats
Elongated exhales of acceptance
due to proper circulation

Otherwise known as, 'blood flow'

Echoes only struggle for existence
in silence
Waiting on unspoken octaves to breach upon
Hung by the lashes of
time-ridden tongues
Through words relevant by
release date

--Reminding one; to grow

But if some mirror takes you down
through a place you left alone
Don't tear your face another hole
Look for fireworks
in the burning pupils
like a tunnel with excitement
on two ends

SURVIVAL

Glow, as if not doing so
would mean
you'd forget how to
by lack of practice
In order to be continued,
one meanwhile
has to be present;
at some point
Future locked itself in Tadasana
Stood still like a statue
in the reach of eager minds
that stretch aspiration
to stitches
Available for aim
So all that ever happens
brings it closer
All you have to do
is move

No Parachute

NAT WHITE

ABOUT THE AUTHOR

Nat has been working closely with Magesoul Publishing for the last two years as a member of the Executive Team, Editor and Home Author. Since 2017, she has actively run and supported various poetry pages as a curator, host of live shows, and is currently co-editor of 'Evolution', Magesoul Publishing's connection to the Instagram community.

To combat the isolation that followed after the two youngest of her four children were diagnosed with autism, this Aussie-born soul reconnected with the world, through words. Her debut collection 'Salted Caramel Tears' was released in October 2019 and she is working on second collection, 'Sage Infused Rain'.

In this chapter, Nat has taken a very different approach to the way she delivers her own journey of survival, providing journal entries in prose that when combined together create an entire story, but when separated are each connected with a piece of poetry, giving a rare backstage pass to the inspiration behind her words.

 @natwhite.au

Forget Me Not

"I once told someone - that I wasn't scared of their demons, it was my own that terrified me. For the most part, I keep them at bay. But louder and louder of late they have cried for my attention... their screeches tearing through my marrow.

Now I know why I feel like I'm surrounded by people - screaming, while no one can hear me. Now I know, the reason I can't escape the screeching - is because my demons, are me."

> The last time
> I was in this place,
> I called three
> of my most important people -
> and *not one* answered the phone.
>
> I then spent seven hours contemplating
> how I could take my own life
> (with the least possible impact upon
> the ones left behind),
> and somewhere in those
> four hundred and twenty minutes or so,
> I came to the conclusion I'd died -
> *a long time ago*.
>
> You can't take a life that doesn't exist.
> My soul, was tired.
> A mere bundle of bone
> aching, *to live.*

SURVIVAL

Today, I'm back in this place,
more exhausted than ever before.
And it just occurred to me,
the reason I feel so bad
is that many of the ones I love most,
consistently reinforce the fact
that I am but a breathing corpse,
begging to be seen, in this...
my cemetery.

That I, can decorate this tomb
with as many flowers as I like,
but it will still be a burial site.

And visitors will only come,
when they remember,
not to forget.

The Hardest Place

"As a small child, I was taught to speak when I was spoken to. Taught, that what is preached is not often practiced. Ruled by doctrine. Controlled by silence. Conditioned by fear. With people leaving. I struggle to believe anyone will stay, because those that should have, didn't. I struggle to believe what people say, because if my life were a movie, the moral of the story would lead one to believe that actions, rarely measure up, to words. I learned this to be the rule, rather than the exception.

"Do as I say, not as I do", was bred into me. Whenever I spoke my truth or had a differing opinion, someone would get mad and I would be punished by words or hands, so I began to please and appease in ways that caused me both physical and psychological harm. I genuinely believed my feelings were not important - and this deluded misconception severely impaired my self-worth and value systems.

While I continued to comply, struggling to assert myself in a positive light, I was forced to juggle a tsunami of emotions building inside. At the mercy of meeting expectations often impossible to attain, the walls I'd tried so hard to maintain, collapsed. Self-betrayal erupting in pain, exploding, in equally intense rage. A tidal wave, that had a tendency to destroy everything in sight - and while valid my reasons may have been, they were cast aside, minimised, and I began to wear the liability for things that were never mine to own.

A new habit developed of apologising - even, when I'd done nothing wrong. An expert at turning the other cheek, I learned to seek the good in all. Ignore my better judgement. Hush my instincts. Conform.

Transforming myself to match the demands of those around me, I became putty in their palms. The reflection in the mirror, a far cry from who I am."

SURVIVAL

Behind these ribs of mine,
lies a heart of anarchy.
A rebel that pays no mind
to the one inside
my skull.

Breaking out beyond
the bones
of the cage
she beats within,
only to jump
into the arms
of pandemonium.

Even now,
older and wiser
and heavily scarred,
she still tries to hold
the types of souls
who don't know how,
to be loved.

But it's come
at a hefty price,
for all too often
I've been left choking
on the rancid taste
of others' regurgitations.

It's amazing how much one can give,
only to be left feeling like a consolation prize.

SURVIVAL

Too many times,
this heart has hoped, has waited
for someone to change,
while they treated her
less like a shrine,
and more, like a grave.

Oh, when will she learn? This heart of mine?

This ridiculously huge, heart of mine.

Sometimes I want,
to seek an intervention.
Call the insane asylum
and have her committed,
this – sponge.
Soaking up the mess
of others' discontentment.
Oozing from the wounds left by
their lashings of resentment.

I think self-discipline
skipped the queue
when it came to me.
I look in the mirror
and see this girl, frantically,
looking for ways
to fix what she can
for anyone else,
as a way to mask all,
she cannot fix, for herself.

SURVIVAL

There are no shortcuts in this life.
You cannot dive off a cliff
and expect not
to break some bones.

And while taking a leap of faith
shouldn't need to come
with a warning label,
I'm the type of girl
who forgets to read
the instructions,
then wonders why,
things fall apart later.

The kind
who will risk driving home
on an empty fuel tank,
for the price of making a difference
in the life of one who may never thank her.

The sort who will try
to resuscitate a goldfish
with a straw,
in hope it can be
resurrected once more.

And as sweet as that may be,
I have come to understand
that sugar is overrated.
A teaspoon of cement
is what I've needed more,
than any other flavour.

SURVIVAL

I had to learn
to let go of my pride.
Stop letting things slide.
No more hiding.
Slap myself hard in the face,
look myself dead in the eye
and say…

*"It is time to stop looking for external distractions
and learn to sit still with your own reflection."*

When it comes to relationships,
there is no easy way to say this…

My track record sucks.

I have a history
that leaves a lot to be desired.

Spent far too long
perfecting the art of contorting
to the whims of temporary admirers.
Gave them an inch,
while they took a mile.
Before I knew it,
they were frequent flyers
while I,
was racking up the mileage.

And because 'out of control' has always been
my most difficult place to be,
I'd kill myself to please, just…
so they didn't leave.

SURVIVAL

Why couldn't I see?

Once depleted,
they'd leave anyway.

Let's face it -
how many stayed,
when I had nothing left to give?

I know, very few.

The time had arrived
for me to disrobe the skeletons
that had my closets bursting
at the seams.

No more skipping
over the important parts,
like I skip over the ugliest of scenes
in scary movies.

And even though it may be true,
that the only arms
that ever felt like home
are the ones that let me go,
I wanted to lean,
to believe.
To have faith
that one would stay.

Yet the thought
of someone doing that,
is still so hard to contemplate.

SURVIVAL

Stay...

The word tastes bitter
like a broken pill
left to linger
on my tongue.
Lodged in the back
of my throat.
Too hard to swallow,
too late to spit out.

What if someone did decide to stay?

How could I ever see another's arms,
as a safe place to go,
when the only ones
I'd ever known
had failed to break my fall?

When the only home I'd ever known,
was a place called 'all alone'?

How could I stop for one moment to face
my own internal hell?

When the hardest place I'd ever had to sit,
was with, myself?

SURVIVAL

No Parachute

"I have a past littered with chaos, trials and tribulations. I've made some terrible choices. Sometimes the same ones. Repeatedly. And despite an innate ability to forgive and do my best to treat others the same as I wished to be treated, 'Love' as a receiver, has always come with conditions.

It has taken a journey I wouldn't wish upon my worst enemy, to grow the compassion that has become an intrinsic part of my DNA. While I recognise I have been blessed in equal measure to my suffering. Bared witness to miracles. Been gifted the honour of motherhood. Looked adversity straight in the eye as I've crawled, then kneeled, then stood. Blow after blow - I've continued to bleed. Carrying wounds that seem to keep weeping - no matter how much I try to sew them closed.

Whilst I am resilient and courageous when the need arises, it is for this very reason I am perceived by many as 'strong', so much so they forget I'm far from invincible. This has forced me to depend solely upon myself, to the point of my own detriment. Scraping the bottom of the barrel for even a shred of support, even though others will often depend and rely on me. I am accustomed to being treated poorly. It is a sad fact that when I am treated well, I question it. My experience has seen this to be merely a temporary measure to enable others to take what they can. Each and every time, leaving me a little more jaded than before. A little more wary. A little more cynical. Critically analytical. Pushing the people that really care away, when what I really need, is for someone to remain.

When I had finally face-planted the ground one too many times, I reached the conclusion the only thing I had power over were my own choices.

SURVIVAL

And when I was willing to confront the arduous task of drowning out the insidious voices inside, in closing my ears, I opened my eyes to see I could not continue to blame myself for the false belief that 'being loved' meant 'fulfilling everyone else's needs but mine'. It became clear that balance and boundaries were the two key ingredients missing, limiting my ability to have healthy relationships. Knowing both of these are my responsibility to uphold, they felt and still feel extremely foreign.

The 'unknown' triggers a different fear. Territory I desperately long to explore, yet step into with trepidation. Always waiting for the other shoe to drop. For the rug to be pulled out from underneath me."

I wasn't always this way, you know.
I used to take everyone at face value.
Believe what I was told.

I never questioned.
Never doubted.

I just jumped right in.
To people.

Headfirst.

No parachute.

And maybe,
I became tired
of the earth
enthusiastically
rushing up to greet
my naivety.

```
SURVIVAL
```

Tired of the dirt,
barren and rock hard,
that welcomed me
with such vigour,
it became embedded between
my teeth.
Lodged grains,
in grazes deep.

Maybe,
I grew tired of chipped enamel.
Grinding on the grit of defeat,
bitter upon my bloodied tongue,
whose mumblings
matched the fumbling
of limbs
scrambling to rise,
a second, third,
fourth, fifth, sixth,
seventh,
time.

Maybe,
the view looking up
from the base of the climb
had become
more vivid in my mind.
Far clearer
than the one from the tops
of the cliffs - insistent
on persistently
encouraging me
to fly.

SURVIVAL

Maybe,
from somewhere deep inside,
I saw how easily
I was blinded by thorns
masked behind
the sweet scent
of the artificial roses
I'd chosen as beds,
in which to bury
my hopeful heart.

Maybe,
that's when fear
took over the driver's seat,
from my incessant urge
to please.
When I became
an expert in the art of
questioning… *everything*.

Swinging the pendulum
in the opposite direction,
after many a period of
self-reflection,
introspection.
The veil lifted,
revealing the major cause
of my injuries,
was simply an inability to accept
the reality
that not everyone
is like me.

```
SURVIVAL
```

Oh, the irony
of the scars
I carry upon this soul.
Invisible to all
but the beholder.
Until they make themselves
known.
Reopening when
I least expect it.
Sutures unravelling
as I panic to seal them shut
before they bleed too much
and are seen -
by the very same eyes
I wish to hide them from.

Oh, the irony
of these battle wounds.
That tell the tales
of what I've survived.
And endured.

How, instead of wearing them
with pride, I try
to diminish their existence.
Overwhelmed by shame
in their persistence
to float to the surface,
in my most vulnerable
of times.

Oh, the irony.

SURVIVAL

That these lacerations,
these imperfections,
can somehow become
the trigger.
The weapon.
The ignition.
The driving force of distrust.
Hesitation.
Alienation of others
undeserving
of such suspicion.

Oh, the irony
of these scars.
These remnants of my past.

Whose mere presence
can influence my present
and impact the outcome
of my future.
Oh, the irony.

And I'm sorry.

Because...

I wasn't always this way, you know.
I used to take everyone at face value.
Believe what I was told.

I never questioned.
I never doubted.

SURVIVAL

I just jumped right in.
To people.

Headfirst.

No parachute.

SURVIVAL

Doors

"Some days it feels like the muscle that keeps me alive has received more beatings than the ones it has taken. Yet somehow, no matter how many times others try to extinguish its light, no matter how many times it's met another's cruelty with a smile, or how many wounds penetrate the surface of its epidermis - it never changes.

Regardless, I was addicted to an existence full of the highest highs and lowest lows. Married to the numbing rush of dopamine and cortisol. Panicking when each hit fulfilled me less than the one before. I found myself at the mercy of a virus, I had to strive to uninstall, but how do you unlock a door, when you never held the key?

In learning to trust myself, the only way to see the difference between a programmed reaction to a trigger and a genuine gut instinct, was by allowing others in. Not everyone, but those who can encourage my growth. Those who can show me, not all have an agenda to take advantage of my good intentions. Those who won't be angry or offended when I speak my mind. Who will not only stay, but will listen, communicate, and compromise. Souls strong enough to call me out whenever warranted - without being unkind.

Those few who have accepted me for all that I am, are helping to recondition me to believe I too am worthy of not only love and forgiveness, but are filling the void of loyalty I've always longed for. Encouraging me to chase my aspirations, make my needs a priority"

You, my Love,
arrived in this world on your own.
You will depart on your own.
You can also survive...*on your own.*

SURVIVAL

Surviving does not always mean
getting it right the first time.
Sometimes it means defying the odds
and reverting back to the not-so-ideal tactics
we were taught long ago.
Sometimes it means falling back
on what we know.

It's rarely pretty.
In fact, it's often brutal.
And in the aftermath,
while wondering
why or how we made decisions
that don't align with our convictions,
we're often harder,
harsher on ourselves,
than the afflictions that put us there.

But once you realise that
we are students
of this universe,
that life will continue to throw
its pupil's lessons - until we pass.

Once you make it through
the dark and see your scars
as simply records of your victories,
you'll be amazed
at the many doors
that will open for you,
and how many,
you'll finally have the courage
to close.

She Said

"We all tote around with us the luggage of our past. All the qualities I am often told are admired are packed inside those suitcases. Right along with souvenirs of scars from battles I have won - and lost. I think we all too often forget our triggers are trophies we should wear with pride, our traumas shields, we must learn to wield, not excuses to hide behind.

If we took apart a kaleidoscope and looked at merely one of its many pieces in the cold harsh light of day, it would not be anywhere near as beautiful. So if you hear who I was, or where I've been, or who you think I am. When you analyse me based upon my 'now' or my 'back then', or see a part of me that you perceive as ugly - it's imperative to know I am not merely one of my flaws nor virtues alone, but the sum of them all.

Some of the unhealthiest decisions I ever made were when I was surviving. Escaping or self-destructing. Avoiding or denying. Aching to be loved or begging to be seen. When we are in that state of mind, we are not always capable of making smart decisions, especially when the options are the lesser of two evils.

We tend to revert to what we've always known when under duress. Bad habits and all. But after the storm, when we find a way to once again stand tall, it is through our struggles that we gain the greatest growth of all. The woman you see today, the one I was before and the one I'll be tomorrow was surviving just like you.

If you want to know what someone is made of, don't scrutinise them solely on how they survived.

Pay closer attention, to how they rise."

SURVIVAL

"You gave everything you had
to those you loved.
Even when you didn't have it to give."

She said.

"You took their rage.
Their pain.
Their problems.
And you held it all."

She said.

"You sacrificed time after time.
Putting everyone first.
Leaving all your own hopes and dreams
to gather dust
on the shelf.
Never to be taken down again."

She said.

"No one saw you.
No one knew how to hold you.
No one believed that you,
of all people,
could fall."

She said.

"You were the strong one.
The '*I'll fight 'til my dying breath*' one.
The '*Never give up on you*'.

SURVIVAL

'I believe in you'.
'You've got this, and I've got you', one.

Without condition.
Without hesitation.

And when your legs gave out
and your spirit caved in.
When you crumbled
under the weight
of all you carried within...
they left.

Nearly everyone
who meant something.
Including me."

She said.

"You shame yourself for lashing out.
For breaking down.
For surviving, the only way you knew how.
You criticise yourself repeatedly
that you could have done better.
That you did not *and were not*... enough.
But it's not all your fault.
There are those who blame everyone
and everything else
and there are others, like you,
who wear the shame of things
that don't belong to them."

She said.

SURVIVAL

"You wear that guilt like a crucifix
and hammer your own
soul to that cross
for the sin of simply being...
human."

She said.

"You were sculpted to be this way.
A by-product of your environment.
A victim of circumstance.
A child, who learned to speak in whispers.
A woman, whose screams remained unheard
by those who had a responsibility
to listen."

She said.

"When it all became too much
and the noise inside your head
became all-consuming
and you wanted to leave.

When the world turned against you,
And you wanted to hide.
You wanted... *to die*.
When all was lost,
against all odds, you...
stayed."

ATTEMPTS AT LIVING A REGULAR LIFE

DAVID JOHN SMITH

ABOUT THE AUTHOR

Born and raised in Massachusetts, David felt the need to write from an early age. He was particularly inspired by New England writers and his family who encouraged reading and creativity.

David often writes of his experiences living with schizophrenia, its daily challenges and occasionally terrifying breaks from reality.

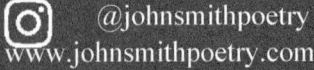 @johnsmithpoetry
www.johnsmithpoetry.com

**A Psalm of David
When He Was in the Desert**

My God, my God,
why have you forsaken me,
forsaken me, my God, my God.

Humanity means that I doubt,
then spit in the face
of my Father.

I walk through the desert
of Reno and Phoenix,
and the sun melts all hope.

Dust sticks to eyelids
and grinds like boulders
into my gums.

My once-upon-a-time friends
have long since gone
to seek something real
without me.

My thirst and hunger
is never satiated,
and the loaves of bread
behind the rocks
leave me weaker than before.

SURVIVAL

My God, my God,
my repentance is great.
My weakness in flesh
has led me in circles.

So close to the end,
I lose sight of what's real.
A second staring at the sun
brings a golden eagle
to my eyes.
The stars grow wings
and butterfly tails.

After, the blur reveals a new design,
but I am too weak, Lord.
I opened my door, finally, to you.
And now the demons
try to claw
through the wood.

My God, my God,
I see eyes everywhere,
but fear that they see
only darkness in me.

(Inspired by Psalms 22 and 63)

That Time I Dialed 911 on Myself

I remember how courteous
the EMTs were
when they arrived at my house.
I sat inside on the stairs,
and they stood in the doorway.

They said something about how
this is the best way,
coming to take me to the hospital
before anything happened.
What could happen?

I found out later that night,
the longest day of my life.
Yes, reality had left me completely.
I dared not describe the wild narratives
that were spinning inside my head.

Waiting in the ER,
I laid down on a stretcher,
and they put a cloth over my head.
I thought, this is a nice way to die.
Maybe if I breathe slower, slower...

And then my arms latched
on to the aluminum caging,
and lightning shot from my hands,
and went downward into the ground,

SURVIVAL

causing an earthquake in Ecuador
that I heard about on the news
three days later.

*Did you know we're living in a simulation
and our brains are attached to a computer
in a floating spaceship?
Oh right, nobody knows this.*

Some hours later,
I walked around a ward
seeing evil spirits embody doctors
looking at me from behind a counter.

I started screaming,
and the strong men came from all over
and picked me up like a corpse.
*They think I'm a vampire,
I'll prove to them I'm holy!*
I dropped down to one knee,
bringing ten men to the floor.

I struggled to the point of exhaustion
while they strapped me down
at the legs, the arms,
and across my chest.

The last thing I remember seeing...
the needles that they tried to stick in me
bent as if my arms were made of steel.

Every Time I Look in The Mirror

Belief is a strange thing.
When I was young,
I believed in God
and all Bible stories,
but also, the scary,
make-believe things
were real as well.

In the hospital room
for thirty nights,
strange women cared for
a toddler in traction,
and the monsters first appeared.

I never slept well after coming home.
I was almost three,
and nobody believed me
or had the tools to catch
early signs of schizophrenia.

Before long,
I stopped sleeping in my bed.
I only felt safe
in the constant presence
of my family,
because when I was alone
I would see glowing faces
with gaping, black mouths,
but nobody believed me.

SURVIVAL

At age five, I first attended school
and began my double identity.
Though I knew with absolute certainty
the rules of this monster-filled world.
(Never be alone
and the monsters can't get you.)
I kept quiet about these things.
I knew the only way to survive
was to act like everyone else.

This brain is a funny thing.
I entered high school,
and the hallucinations
and paranoia
—never treated—
were kept at bay.
I could be home alone,
anywhere alone,
for the first time in my life.

But then
my brain learned a new trick.
The depression and suicidal thoughts
started intensely
when I was about fifteen.

I knew a few things
from years of leading a double life.
Grades were good, friendships stable...
I just wanted,
a little more each day,
for the monsters (that never went away)
to finally get me.

SURVIVAL

By eighteen,
I knew this problem was
all in my head,
and it was getting worse.
I got into a good school,
and won a scholarship
with essays that
made it possible to attend.
But brain disease often gets worse
when left untreated
to fight a daily battle
of not knowing
what's real and what isn't.

I stopped believing in everything,
the only option I had left.
No God. No love. No monsters.

In my freshman year of college,
I confessed to my girlfriend,
"Every day
I think about killing myself."

Imagine putting that on
a pre-med who is
in teenage-love with you.

She somewhat seriously said,
"You should talk to a doctor,"
and we never spoke of it again.
The year went by and we broke up,
but I finally took her advice.

SURVIVAL

I was nineteen and
had just started my sophomore year.
Binge drinking felt like relief,
but in reality only increased
my suicidal thoughts.
One day, as things became
more desperate, I called the college
counseling program,
to schedule an appointment.

I had lived with schizophrenia
for my entire life
in fear, in ignorance,
and in isolation.

I've come to accept
that there is no cure,
one must simply learn
to live with this disease
as best as one can.

I puked this morning,
a side effect of an
increase in medication.
I'm thirty-six now.
I graduated
and built a career.
I've missed
six months of work
out of the last fifteen years
due to illness.

SURVIVAL

Suicidal thoughts
come every hour, it seems.

I have no children,
my elderly beneficiaries
could use the dough.
"I want to kill myself,"
my mind says,
every time I look in the mirror.
No, I brush off the thought.
The sun is shining!
The monsters
peep shyly from the shadows.
Take the medicine with food.
Put on a normal disguise,
and go to work.

SURVIVAL

::::

The Delusions

Today feels like my delusions
are taking over.
I sit in a restaurant by myself
and the old ladies in the booth behind me
are saying my name and
discussing my life story with each other.
I pay the bill,
and walk through crowded streets.
Is everyone looking at me?
Maybe my clothes are old and rumpled.
Maybe my hair is a mess.
I start talking aloud to myself,
then catch it from spreading.
Heads turn in my direction.
Shove the earbuds in,
and pretend I'm on a call.
Almost home, but
this man is following me.
And the children at the playground
are mocking me.
I take a sharp right to lose him.
I turn up the volume
to drown out their screams.
Back to my apartment
with a sink full of dirty dishes
and the hamper stuffed to the brim.
Pull the blinds down
and switch the lights on.

Attempts at Living a Regular Life

Lot of balls in the air
since starting a new job
and new medication.

I haven't watched the news
but once in two months.

I gained back
the twenty pounds I lost,
and there are other
bad habits,
but I try to get out
and walk every day.

Now milk is my enemy,
on a yo-yo diet,
I crash and burn
with french fry fury.

There are people talking about me
at every turn, all day long.
He's doing this.
He's doing that.

Sorry, I just left
in the middle of writing this
to message my doc,
to tell her this stuff isn't working.

SURVIVAL

The little girl across the hall
is terrified of neighbors
checking their mail
in the lobby.

The little girl cries out,
"He's talking to himself!
He's talking to himself!
I hate him!"

God and Miracle Drugs

It's been four years
since that last hospitalization.
I haven't gone back and don't plan to.
Once again, I moved out on my own,
eternally thankful for parents
who took me in and cared for me
every day that I was sick.
I found another job,
and managed to stay clean and fed.

Life moves forward
as the psychosis emerges
and retreats in waves.
I see my doctors regularly.
We haven't had to
adjust the meds in over a year.
I think we found a good regimen.

Every day, I reach out
to someone in my support network
of family and friends
that are aware of my condition.
We talk like regular people,
and I remain attached to something real.

Six months ago,
I met a special woman,
and we're building
our foundation of love.

SURVIVAL

The list of reasons why
I fight to stay alive
keeps growing.
I never would have imagined
such blessings during those
hopeless nights in the desert.
Another day,
another chance to live
—all thanks to God
and miracle drugs.

OPEN WOUNDS

CALLIE CARROLL

ABOUT THE AUTHOR

Callie Carroll, born and raised in Texas, is a woman who is loud on the outside and gentle on the inside. She loves her family, can't live without her friends, and enjoys sports, coffee and the arts. In attempting to find balance while raising her children and starting her own consulting business, she is also passionate about writing and spoken word poetry.

Callie has been writing since high school, but only over the last few years she has found her way back to it and into the Instagram poetry community. Writing is an emotional outlet and comfort for her and she finds it much easier to express herself through written words. Callie is a home author for Magesoul Publishing. She has a few published pieces in other works, as well as two books she is currently working on, and also makes prints of her words against her art.

Callie is currently part of Evolution, Magesoul Publishing's connection to the Instagram community. In addition to being a curator for several pages in the past, she has hosted many Instagram live poetry readings, was a coach for a spoken word season of Poetry Battles, and remains a fervent advocate for the poetry community, kindness, and laughter.

Callie wholeheartedly believes that everyone has a story, their voices should be heard, and that love lives in layers.

 @goingbck2callie

Rise

Some days,
she does not rise with the sun,
when her thoughts become flooded
with the murky waters of memory.

She hears whispers over noise.
Muffled laughter mimics the echo of underwater.
She hears him say "Everclear,"
when thereafter, it all remains never clear.
That which she remembers,
are flashes of visions and sounds.

She can't remember how she got to that room,
but she remembers saying "No!"

She can't remember what he said,
but she remembers saying "No!"

She can't remember the white cotton,
with tiny red and blue flowers, coming off,
but she remembers saying "No!"

She can't remember driving herself home,
but she remembers saying "No!"

She can't remember grieving the loss of what was hers,
and hers alone,
but she remembers saying "No!"

Was it that she was outgoing and bold?

SURVIVAL

A naïve risk-taker, sassy, flirty?
What did it matter?
What does anything else matter?
Other than that she remembers she said "No!"

When her best friend, or
the man she will one day marry, or
the children she will raise
ask
about her first time,
she will say…
"I can't quite remember,
but I remember saying No!"

Some days,
she does not rise with the sun.
Today is not one of those days.
Today, she is the sun.

Delusion

Sweet professions of love.
Powerful proclamations,
of one soul,
separated by two earthly bodies.
Ahhh…
The manipulation of your words,
more cleverly masked than before,
under the deranged delusions
that I don't still have the burns of rage
your fingertips seared into my neck.
That I didn't spend years cauterizing exit wounds
from bullets that flew off your tongue.
That anything you could offer me,
somehow,
would be better,
than you being nothing at all.

SURVIVAL

::::

<u>Pretend</u>

Her soul,
warmer than the mist off the ocean
in the heat of high noon.
Her gaze,
more captivating than the memories
that hold me prisoner.
Her heart,
stronger than a thousand of my hands,
than one hundred of my guns.

She can see my invisible costume of pretend.
Pretend to be unbreakable,
pretend not to care,
so she stays.

She sees what no one else sees,
knows without being told,
because she listens with her eyes.

Her laugh,
a song I've never heard.
Her smile,
a dream in my world of nightmares.
In her presence,
I am otherwise defeated and left weak.
So I protect myself.
Protection is all I know.

I must have my carefully manipulated guard
and my perfectly planned walls,
or she will break in.

SURVIVAL

So I put time limits on our time spent.
I become silent.
I run.
Because the one thing she cannot do;
she cannot run after me.

SURVIVAL

::::

<u>Erosion</u>

Following the breadcrumbs of society,
I walk in desperation,
looking for what I believe to be validation.
When I find the love I have been told to seek,
I see love, I feel love,
believing I have won.

Our foundation is built in passing moments,
on beliefs made of fairytale fabric,
sewn together with the silken thread of evanescent euphoria…
Only the realization awaits,
love alone, is not enough.

I watch
the monotonous rise and fall of life's tide.
The relentless waves of routine.
The cutting winds of the storm,
tossing around dishonesty, temptation and betrayal,
with the weightlessness of that which has no matter;

Eroding our pillars of trust
into rocks that bruise and
sand that is carried away
by the ocean, the wind,
and the feet of passersby.

SURVIVAL

These stones are all I have left to throw,
trying to rebuild my worth,
but instead,
shattering this glass house.

SURVIVAL

::::

<u>Immortal</u>

I walk,
and then I run,
on this path of destruction,
illusioned as a righteous journey,
decorated with flowers
grown from seeds of sin,
planted underneath my skin, and
cut by the blade of your tongue.

And still,
still I run.
Upon mirrored fragments of my reflection,
left in your wake,
ripping flesh from my heels
to bloody my bones.

But I,
I shatter pain's threshold
in this world of demons
wearing your face,
answering to your name,
painting me with the stroke of daggers,
because my love,
though not for you,
is immortal.

Internal

CARLOS MEDINA

ABOUT THE AUTHOR

Known first and foremost as a respected author and published poet, founder and CEO of Magesoul Publishing, Carlos Medina, was born and raised in the Bronx, New York. Sharing most of his talent on Instagram and Facebook, Carlos began his writing journey five years ago after a divorce from a five-year marriage.

Traveling through the deepest crevices of your mind, exploring the passages of your heart, you are able to go into the depths of your soul and experience memories in ways you never did before, thanks to his incredible insight and the way he can captivate you with his gift of weaving words.

In August 2017, Carlos took his passion and created the business that is now known as Magesoul Publishing to help other authors publish their own creations. Having published seven of his own books, the most recent, "Seeking the Unknown" was released in 2019. His ever-growing collection of poetry and prose can be purchased via www.magesoul.com and amazon.com.

  @magesoul   @Magesoul1

  www.magesoul.com   @Magesoul

Preparation

Perhaps the struggles have been hard.
You probably feel like you have hit rock bottom.
You lie down every single night and soak your pillow with tears, wondering,
"Why me? What have I done to deserve this?"
But let me explain something to you, my friend.
You are not alone.
Many have gone through it, and survived.
Your inner strength will rise from within.
I promise you that.
Soon, you will look back and realize
that all these obstacles were actually preparing your soul
for what the future brings.

SURVIVAL

Tonight

Tonight, the sadness of this night will consume me whole. I will think back on everything that we had. I know that is the only way to release this pain I have within. To remember, and to remove every single moment, every day, that we spent together.

I know there is no turning back - that it's all gone, but tonight... tonight, I want to dance with the shadows of my past. Everything that was once a reality is just an illusion now. It hurts, but as each day passes, the pain is felt less. The tears flow, because the truth is, I really did love you. I really did give you my all.

I know that it will never be the same with anyone else because I've learned that as time goes by, as each lesson is accepted, the love and understanding goes deeper. I look forward to that. I look forward to one day showcasing what I have deep within to someone that will appreciate it all.

From the first blink, to the last breath, I look forward to that eternal love.

A Mother's Pain

I witnessed many things at a young age. When I was just seven years old, I saw my step-father leaving for work every day while my mother stayed home and took care of us. One day, she allowed me to go outside and play in the park. As I played with my childhood friends, I looked across the street and saw him looking out the window while he smoked a cigarette. Unfortunately, it wasn't our apartment window. He was two floors down at the window of my Mom's best friend. Being a little boy, I didn't know what to do but cry. I ran straight upstairs and quickly told my mother. I knew that it would hurt her, but I couldn't keep that inside.

As I told her what happened, she couldn't believe it. She was in shock. She quickly took me by the hand and dragged me to her friend's apartment and knocked on her door. She kept knocking and screaming his name out loud, *"I know you're in there, be a man and open the door!"*

Finally, the door opened and his face popped out. She kept banging on the door and yelling, *"Why me? Why are you doing this to me?"* All I could see on his face was embarrassment, and his eyes got watery when he looked down at me.

My mother dragged me back upstairs and sat there on the ledge of the window smoking a cigarette, endless tears running down her face. All I could do was hug her and tell her how sorry I was, because I felt her pain.

SURVIVAL

Thirty-five years later, I still feel it. I still blame myself for telling her what happened, because I know things would've probably been different if I had never said a word. Maybe it was for the best, or maybe it would've been worse. Although I felt her pain and saw her sadness, I can honestly say I have been a witness to her survival.

I witnessed a mother take charge of a household and sacrifice her life for her kids. I've witnessed *that*. I've also lived it. She's my hero. For every battle she has fought, she's come out wiser and stronger. I would go through any level of pain and hell to show her the love I have for her.

A Knock on My Door

I was twenty years old when I decided to sit on that ledge of my window. I felt useless, worthless and that I was not enough for anyone. I was consumed by many thoughts and probably driven by the demons that surrounded me. I sat there for forty-five minutes, looking down from my fourth-floor window. The view was spectacular and a cool breeze was felt. It was perfect to me. Perfect to finally give it all up. To let go of humanity, to let go of those that loved me and to finally see what's on the other side.

I didn't feel fear, there were no tears, if I recall, I couldn't even feel my heartbeat. I felt like this was "it". What felt like an hour was actually just a moment in time. Right before I took that last puff of my cigarette, images of my body on that concrete floor beneath me kept creeping into my thoughts. My parents came into my mind. Thoughts of them crying, thoughts of them blaming themselves for what happened.

I kept moving forward until half of my body was out of the window ledge. The pain was just overwhelming, I couldn't continue living this life. I took many deep breaths, and all of a sudden, someone knocked on my door. I was trying so hard to ignore it. But something kept pushing me back in. A force that, to this day, I can't describe.

I went back into my apartment and checked who was the one knocking. *"Who was the one that interrupted the moment of my departure?"*

SURVIVAL

I opened the door, and the gentleman from church was there. A person I hadn't spoken to in years. He took one look at me and said, "God bless you brother", proceeding to hug me. I welcomed him in and we began to chat and catch up. I tried so hard to fake a smile, to go with the flow, but deep down inside, the pain just wanted to escape my soul.

I sat there, and while he spoke, I began to cry. I couldn't resist the emotions and I just kept telling him, "Pray for me". As the prayer started, I felt a rush within me. A flow of supreme love, a forgiveness from the almighty. I never told anyone what happened that day. I never thought that twenty-two years later, I would realize that I had a purpose in this life. That there was a reason for that individual to knock on my door.

I realize now that we all have a purpose here. It will never be when we want it, but time… time will show you many things. Have patience and believe in yourself. Believe in the things you don't see.

Ashes of My Pain

I've been fighting battles since I was a child. Most of them were protecting loved ones. Few of them were against others, and most of them were against myself. Each battle took pieces of me with them, each one melting my wings in ways I couldn't understand.

I fell into addiction and boosted my ego, all in hopes that I was on the right path. Fortresses were built around my heart, an army of powerful thoughts were constructed just to keep myself on a high and under the illusion of leading a balanced life. What I didn't know was that slowly, I was fading away. I was losing myself to my own shadows. In the process of it all, everyone close to me got hurt.

One day, it was all gone. My marriage, my job, my friends and my sense of self. At that moment I couldn't understand what was going on. Everything that I once had control over, everything, was gone. My beautiful memories became nightmares, everything I had worked for meant nothing. I recall sleeping in my office for a whole week and crying every moment wondering, *"Why me?"... "Why do I have to carry this pain?"..."Why does this life feel so heavy?"*

The following Friday, I looked in the mirror and began to cry. I saw the pain in my eyes, and finally forgave myself. I forgave myself for everything I did. For the hurt I caused. I had to accept that I'm not perfect.

SURVIVAL

That I will make mistakes, and every single day I should remind myself that I've already survived the worst days of my life. I live because I was able to walk through the ashes of my pain, and while those ashes stained my soul, they will be forever remembered as my survival.

In forgiving myself, I opened up the portal within... to allow the beginning of my healing.

In Seasons

CASANDRA ROJAS

ABOUT THE AUTHOR

Casandra Rojas is a Venezuelan writer who grew up in the United States. She speaks English and Spanish fluently, and has been using writing in both languages as a cathartic outlet since her adolescence.

Her writing is mainly inspired by the human condition, her overall perception of life, her struggles with mental health and addiction, as well as her need to find healing, learning, and beauty in the most tragic of situations.

She is a sexual abuse survivor, a single parent, a poet, a spoken word artist and a gentle human sharing pieces of her soul with the world.

The complexity of her use of enjambment, imagery, and metaphors to portray emotion are sure to awaken all the senses, as she leads the reader on a stellar journey through layers of poetic expression.

 @_ohmycas

"The Seed"

Dirt was all I ever knew
I was just trying to find an outlet
that lead to the light
I didn't really know what that was
since I was born in the dark
free to cry and curse
never blessed to begin with
I suppose
being filthy came naturally

...

They say those who carry the world
never shout about it
they don't have the energy
it's a burden held in whispers
and slight grunts of exhaustion

...

Born in a burial ground
of rough diamonds
divinely lost in a graveyard
I want to meet the sky
find grace in the sunshine
get to know it until it burns
unaware that all the stars
are already dead

...

Sweetly longing to seize
the pain of growth

```
SURVIVAL
```

I continue hoping
to become one of them
and if this is my roots taking form
it is impossible to know if they are rotten
  I long to let go and float away
...
Dirt is all I've ever seen
so it is natural
that dirt
is all I have ever done
I say my hands are clean
but all I see
is filled with soiled intentions
(like hate)
and I am unsure why I broke the shell
extending myself into suffering suffocation
digging into the environment with tiny limbs
...
I suppose
it is no surprise that the day
I cracked through the surface
It was raining
and the sun barely blinked in my direction
and the clouds seemed to be the only ones
to acknowledge my presence
washing away of all the mud

"Discovery"

The elements kiss me at dawn
awakening me with all I need
yet I still question purpose
as I extend towards what seems
out of reach
The emptiness surrounding
is not the space I wished to encounter
as I grow into the space between
Gleams in the sky still whisper to me
of being more than what is visible

...

The elements kiss me at noon
and the sun has learned my name
the clouds are still my friends
and the roughness of heat
is still a reason to be grateful

...

The elements kiss me in the evening
tell me stories to keep me living
keep me breathing
while I am sleeping
and I sway with the branches of the trees
as I let them lead me
into discovery
into higher learning
into blessing
into understanding

SURVIVAL

⋮⋮

"The Cold Struggle"

A heart
so cold it burns
is still a loving muscle
it still holds the fires of passion
even if frozen are the flames
even
if
frozen
are
the
flames
...
A stone love is still solid
as it flows through our hands
and bruises our thumbs
and I have made gems out of tears
precious drops of water that fall from
the drought behind my eyelids
not many understand how much these cost
vulnerable despite how hard they land

...
A heart
is still a seed
fragile and resilient
despite its weathered will
and I have seen flowers and garden weeds
stretch root, stem, and leaf from concrete

SURVIVAL

I have seen nature bloom
breaking through brick and marble
as if odds never mattered

...

I have a treasure box full of all the times
I wished upon the shadow of a shooting star
it only looks empty
but it's full

...

I was a child
with a fractured mind
that grew in bits and pieces
pieces that stay in the safety of soil
collecting rocks
collecting dust
becoming comfortable
in darkness and imagination

...

What a dying way to exist

...

I have spent decades ~~seeking~~
retrieving every lost iota
every bit of inconspicuous matter
all I thought dispensable
every last unbearable verity

...

I have been found

SURVIVAL

::::

"Scar Tissue"

There are scars so deep within
that the subcutaneous tissue has no idea they exist
Still
courageous skin is worn like battle gear
Flawed smiles have become crooked medallions
earned in a continuous war alongside soldiers of laughter
that have since become casualties
running through the trenches
of yesterday's disadvantages and lies
she still finds her way
she still finds honesty
...
Blue, purple, and gold ribbons adorn eyes
that have witnessed too much unthinkable atrocity
and even more of simplistic humanity in a filthy society
filled with sequenced scenes that leave viewers sick
and performers uneasy with guilt
...
Not the exception
decades have been spent deciphering contempt and culpability
Contemplating the constellations that have been falling from space
since the first of her kind was named and sold to a Sun god
making for prophetic conversation
...

SURVIVAL

Indefinable worth
undermined by animalistic minds
every single night of savagery
Hers is the daybreak though
as the spells of witching hours fall apart
at the waking of bright deadwood eyes
that fell in love with the way lightning strikes

...

Pummeled in every lifetime
by the same universe
who birthed her
and breastfed her
a millennium of fear
and forgetful counting in reverse

...

Fast forward from behind the curtain
so no soul may notice exactly how it is
jaded teeth were hidden under saccharine lips
that when crescent
the stars would fall to
in admiration.
"Mira!"
they would yell
"A floating body of lost cosmic dust, misplaced."

...

How long ago she must have died
for all to see her ever-going shine
is the question
from intergalactic bodies
that reach down and pin
one more painful prize
on her tired person

...

SURVIVAL

Human
as she adjusts to the steady lessons
Lifetimes
of studying the art of war and defiance
only to learn peace and tolerance

"The Rebirth"

I heard she came to her senses
the broken girl that shattered into womanhood
way before time could give the signal
way before anybody's daughter should

...

I heard she stopped
digging for shrapnel answers
cutting her hands in a sandbox
full of glass concepts

...

I heard the soil was alive regardless of
the non-biodegradable trash buried inside
and I heard she was happier
gardening through garbage treasures

...

They said
the seeds she planted
flowered before spring
I heard it was beautiful
the way roots adhered to earth
and her crops were ready
before the autumn harvest
before expectation

...

and the moon
led their cycle of growth

...

SURVIVAL

more than
the rain, ether, or sun
the moon
led their cycle of growth

BOOKS BY Magesoul Publishing

BOOK I: **IT HURTS**

We have all carried pain.
Some of it spoken.
Much of it buried in silence.

It Hurts brings together fifteen writers who dare to give voice to what so many feel but rarely say aloud. Through poetry, reflection, and raw honesty, each author opens a window into moments of heartbreak, longing, loss, and the quiet struggles that shape us.

Across fifteen deeply personal chapters, these writers transform their most vulnerable emotions into words that echo far beyond the page.

Because sometimes the most powerful thing we can do is admit the truth:

It hurts.

Book II: SURVIVAL

**Pain may break us.
But survival is what defines us.**

At some point in life, every person is faced with hardship. Some wounds are bearable. Others feel impossible to carry.

Yet throughout history, humanity has endured.

We rise.

We rebuild.

We continue.

Survival is a powerful collection of voices exploring what it means to keep going when life tests the limits of the human spirit. Through deeply personal reflections and poetry, these writers reveal stories of resilience, courage, and the quiet strength required to endure.

In uncertain times—when hope can feel fragile—these pages remind us of one undeniable truth:

*The human spirit was built to **survive**.*

Book III: **HEALING**

We all move through phases.
Seasons of breaking.
Seasons of surviving storms we never saw coming. And then-if we are brave enough-there are seasons of healing.

Healing is the final installment of the powerful anthology trilogy by Magesoul Publishing-following It Hurts and Survival.

This collection brings together thirteen courageous writers from diverse backgrounds, each offering deeply personal reflections on trauma, growth, resilience, and transformation.

At its core, Healing reminds us of one powerful truth:
We are not what was done to us.
We are not the sum of our trauma.
We are the ones still standing.
Mending what was shattered. Healing one breath at a time.

More than a book, Healing is a testament to the human spirit. It is a reminder that even after collapse, there can be reconstruction. That even after silence, there can be song. That even after loss, there can be renewal.

You are not alone in your story.
You are not alone in your healing.

And even now, especially now—
you are becoming whole again.

BOOKS BY
Carlos Medina

The Phases of the Soul

Precious Pain

Cremating Past

Eternal Love

Seeking the Unknown

When my Soul Cries

Rebirth (2026)

BOOKS BY
Adric Ceneri

My Poetry: Los Restos de un Humano

Walking Toward Happiness

The Remains of a Human

P E D R O: a novel (November 2026)

Magesoul Publishing BOOKS (By other Authors)

Whiskey Tears – Erica Varela

The Wilted Walls – Kristin L Provenzano

The Side Effects of L – Alex Le'Gare

Timeless Depths – Erica Varela

Anchoring Me – Nicole Hartley

The Side Effects of L – Alexander Le'Gare

Paper Butterflies – Heidi Anne

Piece by Piece – Unknown the Poet

The Trilogy of Anthologies...
Books I, II and III

IT HURTS
SURVIVAL
HEALING

NOW AVAILABLE

www.ingramcontent.com/pod-product-compliance
Lightning Source LLC
Chambersburg PA
CBHW071411070526
44578CB00003B/550